Removing the Veil

What the Old Testament is all about

But whenever anyone turns to the Lord,
the veil is taken away.

(2 Corinthians 3:16)

Dr Charles R Vogan Jr

Copyright © 2001 Charles R. Vogan Jr.
All rights reserved

Scripture taken from the HOLY BIBLE, NEW INTERNATIONAL VERSION, Copyright © 1973, 1978, 1984 International Bible Society. Used by permission of Zondervan Bible Publishers.

ISBN 978-0-6151-5796-2

Cover photo: © Photographer: Pam Roth | Agency: Dreamstime.com

Ravenbrook Publishers

A subsidiary of
Shenandoah Bible Ministries

———— ℘ ————

www.shenbible.org

Contents

Introduction	5
Overview: The Point of the Old Testament	7
Creation	13
The Fall	23
The Covenant	34
The Law	50
The Promised Land	64
The Temple	80
The Kingdom of David and Solomon	101
The Prophets	121
The Importance of the Old Testament	136
A Short Summary of the Old Testament	138

Introduction

It's a shame that, in our day, the Old Testament is ignored so much – almost to the point that we could cut it out of our Bibles and very few people would miss it! There are many reasons for this problem. Probably one primary reason is that the pastors and teachers themselves don't understand it, and *that's* true mainly because *their* teachers didn't understand it.

There are a lot of different theories about what the Old Testament is talking about. Some believe that it's a Jewish book written to and for the Jews, and we Christians therefore have little interest in it. Others believe that it describes the Christian's God too, but in a fundamental, preliminary sense (sort of like a rough sketch in crayon) – these truths are the first things to learn about him. In the New Testament, however, we get the second-level course that we Christians need to understand salvation in Christ, a finished, professional drawing. And of course there are many other theories about the Old Testament as well.

There *is* a way of uncovering the message of the Old Testament – simply use the Bible itself to explain itself. That method has helped me tremendously in understanding what seems to confuse others so thoroughly. For example, this key verse in Paul's letter "cuts to the chase", so to speak, and tells us plainly how to read and use the Old Testament:

> … And how from infancy you have known the holy Scriptures, which are able to make you wise for salvation through faith in Christ Jesus. (2 Timothy 3:15)

Introduction

We don't want to miss plain statements like this. Scholars have a way of dismissing the Bible's own testimony of itself, as if they know the message of the Old Testament better than the naïve, primitive writers of the Bible knew it. This verse, however, claims that the "holy Scriptures" (in Paul's day, that meant the Old Testament) were designed to help us understand "*salvation* through *faith* in *Christ Jesus*" – a concept that we moderns thought was the sole domain of the New Testament!

What we will do here is take a quick tour through the Old Testament and try to see the picture that God is painting. He gave us this book so that we will understand his works better, particularly the works that he did through Christ. If we keep our eyes open for that message, then we will be hearing him speak to *us* in the Old Testament.

I'm convinced that if people really knew what the Old Testament teaches, they would study it with a lot more interest, learn a lot more from it, and begin tying the Old and New Testaments together in a way that would greatly illuminate God and his works. As Paul says, we will become better Christians as we get a better grasp on the Old Testament.

Overview: the Point of the Old Testament

The holy Scriptures, which are able to make you wise for salvation through faith in Christ Jesus.
(2 Timothy 3:15)

Too many books on the Old Testament ignore its own revelation about itself, and (what is more important) they also ignore what the New Testament tells us about the Old. The answers to everyone's confusion about the book are right under our noses. We are, as Jesus complained about the Jewish experts of the Law, missing the whole point.

You are in error because you do not know the Scriptures or the power of God. (Matthew 22:29)

These so-called experts in the Old Testament knew the text inside and out, but they didn't understand its plain message. Of course it was veiled by symbol and type, prophecy and Law; but Jesus seemed to think that they ought to have understood it in spite of the problems. Evidently there are clues on how to read it, principles to keep in mind while reading it that will help us get its true meaning. To press the point home, Jesus claimed that the ancestors of these benighted Jews understood its true meaning!

Your father Abraham rejoiced at the thought of seeing my day; he saw it and was glad. (John 8:56)

So let's gather a few key Scriptures together and find the fundamental lesson of the Old Testament. First, we discover that the Old Testament was veiled to the average person:

> We are not like Moses, who would put a veil over his face to keep the Israelites from gazing at it while the radiance was fading away. But their minds were made dull, for to this day the same veil remains when the old covenant is read. It has not been removed, because only in Christ is it taken away. Even to this day when Moses is read, a veil covers their hearts. But whenever anyone turns to the Lord, the veil is taken away. (2 Corinthians 3:13-16)

The Old Testament contained a mystery – it was the eternal message of God to man, but it was temporarily shrouded in physical dress. The Jews were selected out of all the nations on earth to learn the truth about the only God. But they had a severe problem on their hands: whereas the "gods" of other nations were easy to see (since they were idols of wood and stone and metal), the Jewish God was invisible. In fact, they were not allowed to represent him in any way with the things of earth! (See Exodus 20:4-5 for this command.) So how does one find out what an invisible God is like? The way that God chose is typical of a good educator: he used pictures to teach them.

> In the past God spoke to our forefathers through the prophets at many times and in various ways. (Hebrews 1:1)

Through the events of history, and the great personalities of Israel, God taught them how to be saved from sin and death. This is, after all, the great need of mankind, and the Old Testament teaches us this fundamental lesson in "story book" fashion. The fascinating thing about this is that we Christians can now look back through the Old Testament and recognize our New Testament doctrines all through its stories! Obviously God had the big picture of salvation in view when he laid out the events of

Israel's history in his plans. In other words, he gave the Jews the first version of the story of Christ.

That means that the two books – the Old and the New Testaments – tell the *same story*. The first version was told to a people living in the middle of a wicked, ignorant world; the Israelites needed help to understand a God they couldn't see. After the story was told completely over their 2000 year history, it then went into its second version in the New Testament. Now that we have learned the plot of the story, God is going to lift us Christians up to the spiritual reality that the first version of the story pointed to.

I hope you can see by now that God knew that without that first physical version of the story, we would never understand the second spiritual version. It's like reading a map. If we first study the map before we go somewhere, we will recognize the real roads and terrain when we get there. The Old Testament was the map for our New Testament real-life experiences in Christ.

God didn't always tell the Israelites what was going on behind the scenes. He deliberately kept much of it a secret, a "mystery," to be revealed at a later date, and only through faith. *We* know what he was doing back then, because we have plain statements about it in the New Testament. But still there was something about the Old Testament system that should have made the Israelites wonder what it was really about! For instance, when God told them to build a tabernacle in which to worship him, he said this:

> Then have them make a sanctuary for me, and I will dwell among them. Make this tabernacle and all its furnishings exactly like the pattern I will show you. (Exodus 25:8-9)

But Solomon, after he had built the permanent Temple in Jerusalem, knew that an earthly structure (no matter how glorious) couldn't hold the eternal God:

> But will God really dwell on earth with men? The heavens, even the highest heavens, cannot contain you. How much less this temple I have built! (2 Chronicles 6:18)

Some of them knew (through faith – they could see the spiritual reality looming right behind the physical lesson) that God's Temple is actually in Heaven, and the earthly copy was to introduce the Israelites to the worship of God the easy way.

> They serve at a sanctuary that is a copy and shadow of what is in Heaven. This is why Moses was warned when he was about to build the tabernacle: "See to it that you make everything according to the pattern shown you on the mountain." (Hebrews 8:5)

We Christians know, from the extensive descriptions in particularly Paul's letters and Hebrews, that the Temple and its sacrificial system is a great description of Christ and his sacrifice. Do you see where we are going with this? Without saying as much, the Old Testament story describes Christ and his work in great detail. The Jews had inside information about Jesus long before the rest of the world did. The name "Jesus" was never written in any of the stories, and only once in a while was there a clue that all of this referred to the Messiah to come. Basically God kept telling his people, "Trust me – you'll see all of this later and it will make perfect sense then."

In fact, every story of the Old Testament has this great aim in view: ***to describe Jesus Christ, and our relationship to God the Father through him.*** Christians have always known that there is a lot of prophetic material about Christ in the Old

Testament, and a few symbols and types here and there. But back up another step. The very history of the book, the lives and characters portrayed there, the forces and dynamic flow of the principles involved, all help to complete a grand unified (and very detailed) picture of Jesus and his work. By the time we get to the New Testament, we should already know all about him. The only thing left to be done is to lift our eyes to the spiritual level that the physical pointed to.

> The Law is only a shadow of the good things that are coming – not the realities themselves. (Hebrews 10:1)

In fact, the writers of the New Testament purposely refrain from going over the same material that was in the Old Testament. They figured that you have already done your homework and are ready for the next level – or at least you *should* be.

> We have much to say about this, but it is hard to explain because you are slow to learn. In fact, though by this time you ought to be teachers, you need someone to teach you the elementary truths of God's word all over again. You need milk, not solid food! (Hebrews 5:11-12)

Following this complaint, the writer of Hebrews lists a number of doctrines that we should already be familiar with – truths first learned in the Old Testament. This is also why Paul was so certain that we can learn all we need to know about salvation through Christ by studying the Old Testament, as we have already seen. (2 Timothy 3:15)

The New Testament is a highly condensed, complex description of Christ. Now that we're on a spiritual level, there is much more to learn about him and incorporate into our lives if we're to be ready for Heaven. But *are* we ready? To fully appreciate these higher spiritual truths, we have to be well-grounded in the fundamental truths about Christ. Jesus is the foundation of the entire Church, Old and New Testament. He has thousands of functions in God's Kingdom, and scores of names that describe his personality and works. Many things about him are best described by looking at real-life experiences in people's lives. In light of all this, no wonder that God chose to fully tell the story about him over a period of 2000 years, through the lives of millions of people, across a book that makes up fully ¾ of our current Bible! It couldn't be done in a shorter span.

And it can't be sidestepped without great harm to one's understanding of who Christ is. Christians who don't know anything about the Old Testament are crippled in their understanding of Christ. It's true that they may have the germ of salvation in their minds (and hopefully their hearts), but that's because God is merciful and works with us according to our circumstances (which in these lean spiritual times will mean ill-equipped Christians). The problem is that we are Gentiles who have been brought into a new world, a world that only the Jews have had any formal training in. God made us alive in Christ, it's true; but with *only* that feather in our cap we can hardly claim to be experts on God and his Word! Now is the time for training, and teaching, so that "we all reach unity in the faith and in the knowledge of the Son of God and become mature, attaining to the whole measure of the *fullness* of Christ." (Ephesians 4:13)

So our goal here is to ask the question: What does the Old Testament teach me about Jesus Christ? If we keep that question before us as we read it, we will be looking for the right lesson in its pages, the one thing it was designed to teach us. We will be turning our ears and hearts to God, who wants to tell us this very thing. Aiming at any other goal while studying the Old Testament is missing its point.

Creation

It is I who made the earth and created mankind upon it. My own hands stretched out the heavens; I marshaled their starry hosts. (Isaiah 45:12)

The first story of the Bible is about Creation. This is for a very good reason: here we learn about what kind of a God we have, how he works, what he is after, and what he expects of us.

A good introduction sets the tone for the rest of the book. And a really good book will have the germs of all the main points of that book in its introduction. The Genesis account of Creation does this very thing.

The Creation story appears, on the surface, as a simple account of how God created the world. But it's possible to miss the bigger picture (which it seems that many in our day have missed, since there's such a fierce debate raging over what it means!) – which is that the Creator God of Genesis is also our Savior, and he uses the same methods in the Second Creation that he used in the First Creation.

The three methods of Creation

First, let's look at the three methods that God used to create the world.

God created the world through his *Word*. In a number of verses in Genesis 1, it says that "God said" – which means that he spoke the world into existence. You will find that whenever God does something he first speaks it – his Word precedes and surrounds his works. This is a critical piece of information for our understanding of God.

Creation in particular is a good case study in this regard. Left to our own devices, we would no doubt explain the origins of the universe through scientific theories – evolution, for instance, and the Big Bang of physics. The problem is that this approach paints a very definite picture of what God would therefore be like – a weak, disinterested God who lets the world run on its own without much intervention from him. And scientists are quick to jump to those conclusions. In the words of one famous modern physicist, modern science has so well explained the workings of the universe that it appears that "there is nothing left for a Creator to do." That is, the world makes itself, runs by itself, and takes care of itself; it doesn't need God.

Since God's sole aim is to get glory, this state of affairs won't do. He wants credit for what he did. So when he gives us his account of how he made the world, he's going to reveal to us what really happened. To *reveal* something means to make it plain to us, so that there's no mistake about what really happened. So he first speaks his intention of Creation, he describes to us what he is doing and how he does it, so that there is no mistaking his meaning. We have from his own mouth a description of the Creation process, step by step, in Genesis 1.

There's something that happened during Creation that we can never know apart from God showing us. None of our reasoning, or our scientific principles, or our instruments would ever be able to pick it. The methods that God used are completely hidden from our view until God pulls the veil away and shows us plainly – which is what he does here in Genesis.

This is critical to get. God reveals himself and his works to us; we can't understand them until he does. Without that revelation we would draw the wrong conclusions about God. We cannot overemphasize how important this idea is. If God wanted to create the entire universe in an instant, he could have easily done that. But rather than leave us guessing about how he did it, he slowed the process down and described it to us step by step. And what he primarily wanted us to learn about how he created the world are the next two steps.

God created the world through *miracle*. Any child who reads the Genesis creation account will tell you that God used miracles to make the world. When God speaks and something just appears, that's obviously a miracle.

But let's be careful to define a miracle – because we're going to need a rigorous definition as we proceed through the rest of the Bible which describes even more miracles. A *miracle* is when ***God does something directly by his own hand, apart from natural means***. Man has his own way of accomplishing things; he understands the process of getting from point A to point B because he studied it and worked it out. But when God does a miracle, he jumps from point A to point B without using any steps in between. For example, when we make bread we go through a number of defined steps to our goal: from the seed to the harvested grain to the flour to the finished loaf. But God made bread without any intermediate steps – he simply spoke it into existence (remember the manna in the wilderness).

When God made the world, he *had* to do it by miracle; there was nothing there in the beginning to work with!

> Now the earth was *formless* and *empty*, darkness was over the surface of the deep, and the Spirit of God was hovering over the waters. (Genesis 1:2)
>
> By faith we understand that the universe was formed at God's command, so that what is seen was not made out of what was visible. (Hebrews 11:3)

So there was a distinct jump from nothing to something; God's Word has the power to create a world out of emptiness.

Again, this is clearly seen in the miracles of the rest of the Bible, and particularly in the miracles of Christ. He did impossible things simply by speaking them into existence. He changed water to wine (a perfectly natural process, if you give Nature at least six months and good soil to do it with!) with no intermediate steps. He healed incurable diseases and raised the dead with no assistance from medicines or powers of this world. What this shows us, again, is that Christ is the Creator, doing only what God can do, doing necessary things that the world and all of its power can't do. Because of the Genesis account, we now know who to call on when we need something that the world can't give us! See for example Hezekiah calling on the Creator God to save him from his enemies – *now*, in a *miraculous* way. (2 Kings 19)

God created the world through *command*. The Hebrew word behind each of the phrases "Let ... appear" or "Let there be ..." is in the form of a command. God commanded each thing into existence. This has tremendous consequences on our world, if you can see them.

If God commanded the world's existence, that means several things. **First**, God is obviously the King who rules over the entire universe. We all belong to him, he made us, and he will arrange and dispose of everything as he pleases. **Second**, when a King commands something, what he expects is obedience. That makes every one of his creatures his *servants*. We were made solely to serve him, to carry out his will. We have no other purpose in life. As soon as we popped into existence, we found ourselves face to face with our King who demands our obedience.

Third, the entire issue of morality is founded on the commands of creation. We now know what right and wrong are – right is what the King expects of us, and wrong is what the King said not to do. It's very simple.

Fourth, a king expects to see certain things from his subjects, and there must be a day of reckoning to make sure those things happen. In God's case, Judgment Day was on the schedule of the universe the first day it was made. If we did what he told us to do, there will be reward; if not, then there must be punishment. Judgment Day is absolutely necessary to round out the entire scheme of Creation – there must be an accounting. The Creator must determine if the world he made is measuring up to what he wanted it to be. If so, he will keep it; if not, he must destroy it and redo it.

Now these are obvious elements of the Creation account. Let's make the obvious connection, then, to Christ himself. What this story tells us is that Jesus will use the same methods to create not only the physical world, but his new spiritual kingdom as well. In the Gospels we watch him use these very same methods – he is evidently the Creator God at work, doing the *same work* in the *same way* as he did at the beginning. Take most any story of the Gospels and you will see all three of these methods: his Word, a miracle, and a command. No wonder, then, that Jesus himself claimed to be doing his Father's work!

> Jesus gave them this answer: "I tell you the truth, the Son can do nothing by himself; he can do only what he sees his Father doing, because whatever the Father does the Son also does." (John 5:19)

Jesus the Creator

When we watch Jesus at work in the Gospels, it's plain that the Creator has come to earth in person. He uses the very same methods there that he did in the beginning! Jesus spoke his *Word*, he worked *miracles*, and he *commanded* – and through these means he ruled over his Kingdom on earth. As he said, we can tell that he is from the Father because he did the same works that his Father did. One of the clearest examples of all three principles at work is in the story of Jesus raising Lazarus from the dead.

Jesus called in a loud voice, "Lazarus, come out!" (John 11:43)

Why is it important to realize that Jesus is the Creator? There are two reasons. **First**, he has to have such power and authority over the first Creation that he can destroy sin and its effects. "The reason the Son of God appeared was to destroy the devil's work." (1 John 3:8) And that's exactly what we see in his ministry, as he tackled sin and its destruction head on. He has the authority to name sin and rebuke it; he undoes the effects of sin – misery, destruction and death; and he lays the ax at the root of sin so that it can't continue to destroy his people. For such work he needs absolute power and authority over the world, as he claimed several times:

All authority in Heaven and on earth has been given to me. (Matthew 28:18)

But take heart! I have overcome the world. (John 16:33)

Second, and this is the amazing part, *he himself* will lead the first Creation through death and resurrection into the second Creation. The first Creation is doomed to destruction, because of the sin and death that entered the world at the beginning. We need a new model, a new world, and a new nature because the old nature is no good anymore. That model is Christ: we know what we *will* be by looking at what he is *now* after his resurrection from the old world to the new world.

The world itself, as well as the sons of God, wait for the day when the old Creation will be shaken out (Hebrews 12:26-27) and we will be made new in the image of the Son of God who rose from the dead as a spiritual man:

Creation

> The creation waits in eager expectation for the sons of God to be revealed. For the creation was subjected to frustration, not by its own choice, but by the will of the one who subjected it, in hope that the creation itself will be liberated from its bondage to decay and brought into the glorious freedom of the children of God. We know that the whole creation has been groaning as in the pains of childbirth right up to the present time. Not only so, but we ourselves, who have the firstfruits of the Spirit, groan inwardly as we wait eagerly for our adoption as sons, the redemption of our bodies. For in this hope we were saved. (Romans 8:19-24)

> For since death came through a man, the resurrection of the dead comes also through a man. For as in Adam all die, so in Christ all will be made alive. But each in his own turn: Christ, the firstfruits; then, when he comes, those who belong to him. (1 Corinthians 15:21-23)

And in what Paul calls a mystery, Christ represents in his own body the passage of the first Creation to the second Creation. The first physical kingdom will change into a new spiritual kingdom; the King himself puts his physical body to death (the first Creation must be put aside) and then leads his subjects into a new life. That new life is what we will be like, if we join ourselves to him. So, he became one with us physically so that we could become one with him spiritually.

> Since the children have flesh and blood, he too shared in their humanity so that by his death he might destroy him who holds the power of death — that is, the devil — and free those who all their lives were

held in slavery by their fear of death. (Hebrews 2:14-15)

So will it be with the resurrection of the dead. The body that is sown is perishable, it is raised imperishable; it is sown in dishonor, it is raised in glory; it is sown in weakness, it is raised in power; it is sown a natural body, it is raised a spiritual body. If there is a natural body, there is also a spiritual body. So it is written: "The first man Adam became a living being"; the last Adam, a life-giving spirit. The spiritual did not come first, but the natural, and after that the spiritual. The first man was of the dust of the earth, the second man from Heaven. As was the earthly man, so are those who are of the earth; and as is the man from Heaven, so also are those who are of Heaven. And just as we have borne the likeness of the earthly man, so shall we bear the likeness of the man from Heaven. (1 Corinthians 15:42-49)

Finally, we know that his resurrection into a new Creation was planned *before* the first physical Creation. Obviously God had all this planned out from the very beginning. Therefore Creation was the first step to an overall plan which included Christ's physical life, death, resurrection, and our union with him to form a Second Creation.

He was chosen before the creation of the world, but was revealed in these last times for your sake. (1 Peter 1:20)

,,, the Lamb that was slain from the creation of the world. (Revelation 13:8)

To summarize, the world was made *through Christ* because, **first**, it must be totally under his control. **Second**, he intends to destroy it completely, because as it stands – under the effects of sin and death – it can't continue on into eternity in God's plans, nor can it contribute anything of value to a new, eternal, spiritual kingdom. **Third**, when the time is ripe (and in himself he already took the first step) he will do away with the physical creation that we are familiar with and replace it with a perfect spiritual Kingdom. The entire universe then is a kingdom in which Christ is working out his own agenda, from beginning to end.

The Fall

God made mankind upright, but men have gone in search of many schemes. (Ecclesiastes 7:29)

In stark contrast to the positive, upbeat note of God's Creation, the story of the Fall of mankind casts a shadow over all of human history. We all know that there is a problem in the world; but again, because of the revelation given here in Genesis, we now know the exact nature of the problem and its true scope.

In Genesis 3 we are introduced to the problem and its basic elements. The story is that Satan led Eve to believe that God wasn't being entirely honest in his dealing with his new humans. According to Satan, it was almost as if God was deliberately denying them a privilege and pleasure that they had a right to! Finding that this line of reasoning struck a resonant chord in her own feelings and desires, she broke God's command and ate from the Tree of the Knowledge of Good and Evil. Then she gave some to her husband Adam and he also ate it. From this time on, their "eyes were opened" and they became sinners, rebels against God, and shut out from the Tree of Life as well as from Paradise.

The elements of sin

The first sin also shows us the true nature of sin. Let's look at the main elements and discover what really happens to all of us when we sin against God.

- **The nature of sin** – Sin is, at bottom, rebellion against God's commands. God plainly told Adam and Eve to not eat the fruit of the Tree of the

Knowledge of Good and Evil. It isn't recorded that he told them why, but only that he commanded it.

There are a lot of definitions of sin in the world. Some claim that sin is selfishness; others that sin is not being patriotic, or not showing love toward others, and so on. In fact, one of the most confusing aspects of the whole subject of ethics and morality is that every person, and every institution, has their own standard of what is right and wrong. Usually each person thinks himself or herself to be basically good, and has strong feelings about how others aren't doing the "right" thing!

But how can each person's personal standards of right and wrong be correct when none of us agree? If I think that it's "right" to do such and such, when someone else thinks that that same action is "wrong" – who is in the right? Who is to judge? Even our own society changes the rules from generation to generation; what is considered acceptable behavior in our day would have gotten someone a prison term or a beating a century ago!

Fortunately we don't have to guess about what is right and wrong. As we've already seen, God the Creator has designed his world to run a certain way – and that defines what is right and wrong. He commanded the world to obey him; any deviation from his will, design and command is wrong. Man, too, is obligated to do exactly what his Creator designed him to do, and do what's expected of him as ruler over God's earth.

When man turned his back on God's command, therefore, he was introducing a new concept in the Kingdom: rebellion against the King. Man, the pinnacle of God's Creation and the Lord's representative on earth – the one through whom all the earth would know and experience the love and rule of God – separated himself from his Master. From now on, man will rule himself; he is no longer interested in God's will. This is the root of sin.

> Everyone who sins breaks the Law;
> in fact, sin is lawlessness. (1 John 3:4)

And it still is. Even the nicest people you have ever met have no intention of finding out God's will for their lives, or carrying it out completely so that he might be glorified. Sin not only has its ugly side (murder, rape, stealing, lying, etc.) but it is also quite simply not carrying out God's program in his Creation as we were first designed to do. For this we will be judged and condemned as sinners, rebels, destroyers of his Kingdom.

God cannot allow even the least sin in his Kingdom. Sin destroys; it dishonors God and tears down the world he made. Sin disrupts the fine balance of Creation. Whereas every detail in the world was tuned to perfection – every part would do its job perfectly in the system, and bring God the glory that it was fully capable of – sin introduces a fatal flaw in that perfect system that will result in everything falling apart and failing its Maker.

When a minor servant disobeys a command, it's bad enough – and he must be punished for his rebellion or others will get the idea that it's OK to rebel. But when the ruler himself goes bad, he takes the whole world with him into rebellion and ruin. It's the most disastrous thing that could have happened. The entire world is now corrupted because of Adam and Eve's sin.

If we need proof of the ruin that this one single sin brought upon the world, Genesis 4-11 gives it to us. Even the children born of sinners are murderers in their hearts. They raise their fists against God the King around the world. People of every language and culture rebel against God. The world is so bad that God's judgment of them is fearsome:

> The LORD saw how great man's wickedness on the earth had become, and that every inclination of the thoughts of his heart was only evil all the time. The LORD was grieved that he had made man on the earth, and his heart was filled with pain. (Genesis 6:5-6)

By the time we get to the end of the description of sin and its results in Genesis 11, we are wondering if there is any hope for mankind.

- **The work of Satan** – The history of Satan isn't well known. We are fairly certain that he used to occupy a high place in God's Kingdom, and was thrown out of Heaven for his own rebellion against God's throne. We read of him in the book of Job where he tried to get God to curse Job. But we get enough information about him in Genesis 3 to be fully aware of his work among us, here on earth.

Satan's **goal** is our destruction; that is plain. Knowing the curse of God against sinners, he did his best to lead Adam and Eve into that destruction. He is a murderer; he can and will use any method at all to kill us, physically and spiritually. In fact, when we think that our own wars and revenge killings are serving *our* interests, it's not unlikely that Satan is, behind the scene, achieving *his own* goal of wiping out as much of the human race as he can through our efforts of destruction. This serves his purpose of denying us the gift that he can't have – to live with God (as we were supposed to at the beginning) and to enjoy him forever.

> You belong to your father, the devil, and you want to carry out your father's desire. He was a murderer from the beginning. (John 8:44)

Satan's **method** is to lie to us, to deceive us and get us to believe anything other than the truth of God. His statement to Eve was mostly the truth, with a little twist in it that deviated from the truth. He deliberately denied that God would put them to death: "You will not surely die."

> You belong to your father, the devil, and you want to carry out your father's desire. He was a murderer from the beginning, not holding to the truth, for there is no truth in him. When he lies, he speaks his native language, for he is a liar and the father of lies. (John 8:44)

Satan wanted to achieve two things here: *first*, to get Eve to doubt the Word of God. Always, the devil's aim is to steer us away from the Truth of God to believe anything else, it doesn't matter what. Only the Word of God has life in it; so Satan will lead sinners to believe and trust in anything but the Bible – or, if he can't take us away from that, he will pervert our understanding of the Bible and have us believe that. *Second*, he wanted to deceive Eve about the real outcome of the matter, that she was in no danger if she ate of the fruit.

There's a phrase in the New Testament that reveals a hidden but dangerous aspect of sin:

> But encourage one another daily, as long as it is called Today, so that none of you may be hardened by *sin's deceitfulness*. (Hebrews 3:13)

Sin is deceptive; it misleads us by not showing us the entire truth. Like a worm dangling on a hook, or a piece of cheese tempting a mouse onto a trap, the temptation to sin leads us into a hidden but open door to death.

The deceit, the lie that the devil was using here, is common to all temptations: ***you can do this and get away with it!*** Nobody will know. Nothing bad will happen. That's the lie that often makes the difference with us and coaxes us into the forbidden area. Between making the sin attractive, and hiding the dark threat behind the scenes, we fools reach out and take what is offered with the vain hope that it will be good – a rose without thorns. A little thought beforehand about the way God made his world to run would undeceive us very quickly, but sinners typically rush in without thought – or, what is worse, doubting that God's threat is real. And so we fall prey to the trap.

- **The wrath of God** – God *did* promise Adam and Eve that, in the day that they ate of the Tree of the Knowledge of Good and Evil, they would die. They probably didn't understand the severity of the punishment, however.

Physical death started working on them the moment they disobeyed him. The clock started ticking in their bodies: they and their children were now doomed to get sick, suffer physical ills, fall prey to accidents, endure the lack of food and drink, lie under the wrath of the elements around the world as the earth convulsed and heaved under the wrath of God cursing his Paradise into a hard and troublesome earth.

I'm convinced that man lost many of his powers over Creation, abilities that God had given him to rule over the world and maintain the necessary balance of life. Animals now fear him, for the most part, instead of subjecting themselves to him. The only thing that we can do with most of them now is kill and destroy them, not control and rule over them. Mind experts tell us that we're not using anywhere near all of our brains – doesn't this point to potentially amazing powers of mental skill and strength in the first created couple, especially in light of their responsibilities over the earth? One of the first acts of man after his creation was to name all the creatures; because we use names to accurately describe things, this points out Adam's keen intellect to know the true nature of each creature. In other words, what we have now, intellectually, are only the vestiges remaining from an awesome mind, weak shreds reminiscent of a former glory.

And when Adam died, the world witnessed a horrible reality: God kept his promise that the man would not be allowed to live on in his sin. Man was never meant to die. Man's death is an unspeakable tragedy – someone bearing the image of God falls, suffers and dies instead of living with God.

Life is the ability to experience. And the things that Adam and Eve experienced in this world was the world itself, the gift that God gave them to enjoy. Death is God taking away the ability to experience this physical gift – a punishment for their hard-hearted rebellion.

Spiritually speaking, Adam and Eve died immediately upon their rebellion. Man is not just a body, but soul and spirit as well. He has two natures within him: the physical side that experiences physical realities, and the spiritual side that experiences God directly.

If life is the ability to experience, then spiritual life is experiencing God.

> Now this is eternal life: that they may know you, the only true God, and Jesus Christ, whom you have sent. (John 17:3)

God himself is Spirit, and he made man capable of knowing him. This is fitting, again, in light of the responsibilities that he gave man – to rule the earth in God's Name, according to God's will and power. In order to carry out this directive, man had to be able to be in constant touch with God to find out his will. There are also vestiges of this old ability in our minds, since strange mental contacts and abilities to communicate with the spiritual world have been documented in history. The thing to remember is that these mental doors were once open into Heaven's throne room to report for duty; now they open instead into a dark world where any evil spirit can play with us to destroy us.

When Adam rebelled, God cut off his access to Heaven, effectively isolating him in spiritual darkness on earth. Now Adam can't approach God, he can't find him, he can't hear him anymore, he doesn't know his will – he's entirely on his own now. Notice that God had to come find him in the Garden to speak to him, because Adam was hiding in the trees – that former communion was lost.

All of Adam's children are also born into this spiritual darkness and isolation. Being cut off from God is spiritual death; we are all born into it when we enter this world. If there's ever going to be any knowledge of God from now on, it will be by another route instead of by a direct awareness through our minds.

Man makes his own world

There's one more tragic aspect of the fall of mankind into sin. Remember that when God made the world, he declared it to be "good." This means that he was satisfied with the way he made it. Can man improve on God's works, which were guided by unlimited wisdom and goodness? Hardly! So man's responsibility was to maintain that world in its goodness, to keep the fine balance of all its elements. Considering how large the world is, and how small man is, that would be a lifetime job!

But when Adam and Eve turned their backs on God and their responsibility to him, they found themselves cut off from God's wisdom and will. Now what will they do with this world that God cursed with thorns and hard labor? Well, they're going to remake the world to suit them! So now they, in concert with the devil, are "creating" a world that will give them the pleasure and ease that they want from it. They twist and pervert, they destroy and kill, they tear down and build up. They make artificial pleasures, artificial homes, artificial protection. They "improve" the quality of life and suffer the technological consequences of their "improvements."

Now we have a world of our own creation, a complex mess actually, that gets worse from generation to generation. It's all a result of man thinking that he could and should change God's original design to suit his own passions and glory instead of God's glory.

Judgment

There are many people who think God would never punish (that is, to destroy) people for their sins. Least of all do they believe in an eternal punishment like Hell. Since we read in the New Testament that "God is love," how could anybody think that God would be so cruel as to submit human souls to eternal damnation?

The story of the Flood in Genesis 6-8 should be a plain enough statement on what God will do when he's aroused in anger. As the passage states, he was disgusted with men and women all over the planet because of their wickedness.

> The LORD saw how great man's wickedness on the earth had become, and that every inclination of the thoughts of his heart was only evil all the time. The LORD was grieved that he had made man on the earth,

and his heart was filled with pain. So the LORD said, "I will wipe mankind, whom I have created, from the face of the earth– men and animals, and creatures that move along the ground, and birds of the air– for I am grieved that I have made them." (Genesis 6:5-7)

The Lord destroyed *all living things* by means of the Flood. The only ones who escaped were Noah and his family, and that was because of his faith in God. We are supposed to come to grips with the terrifying wrath of an angry God, who would rather every human being be destroyed than that he should be dishonored and ignored. He can, and will, and does, destroy sinners; as Proverbs 1:7 tells us, *the fear of the Lord* is the beginning of wisdom. He will not tolerate sin.

The Covenant

*What then shall we say that Abraham, our forefather,
discovered in this matter?
(Romans 4:1)*

The promises of God, which we hold so precious, are based on an agreement between God and man that is inflexible, rock-solid, and eternal. We can and must depend on this agreement and his faithfulness to it for our salvation; it is our only hope.

The very salvation that we New Testament Christians rely on is based firmly on the agreement that God made with Abraham; as Paul says, "He is the father of us all." (Romans 4:16) In fact, God made this agreement of salvation *only* for Abraham and his descendants. Only if we can prove that we are the spiritual children of Abraham will we be allowed into the presence of God!

A Covenant

In our day we use contracts and lawyers and courts to make agreements with each other, and we have all sorts of ways to make the other party keep their side of the bargain. But in the days of Abraham they had none of these things; so they had to use a different system for making agreements.

The "covenant" was simply a legally binding agreement between two people. In it they agreed to do certain things for each other. But the Hebrew word for "covenant" is *berith* (Hebrew ברית) and it's used with the word "to cut." There is an amazing reason for this. When two people wanted to make this kind of agreement, they would get some animals and, with a sword, cut them into halves and lay the halves out on the ground, making a path down between them. Then one person would walk down the path between the animal halves and declare what he agreed to do for the other person. The idea was that if he failed to do as he agreed, the offended party would have the legal right to take a sword and do to him what was done to the animals! Then when he was finished making his promise, the other person would do the same. As you can imagine, people didn't enter into an agreement like this unless they were serious about it!

Now turn to Genesis 15 for an example of how a covenant was done. In it the Lord instructs Abraham to cut a heifer, a goat and a ram into halves and lay them out on the ground in two rows. Then when Abraham was put into a deep sleep (so that he could see the Lord come down in a vision), the Lord himself walked down through the animal halves and declared his agreement with Abraham.

> When the sun had set and darkness had fallen, a smoking firepot with a blazing torch appeared and passed between the pieces. On that day the Lord made a covenant with Abram and said, "To your descendants I give this land, from the river of Egypt to the great river, the Euphrates — the land of the Kenites, Kenizzites, Kadmonites, Hittites, Perizzites, Rephaites, Amorites, Canaanites, Girgashites and Jebusites." (Genesis 15:17)

What is truly amazing is that the Lord was submitting himself to the hands of Abraham in this agreement; he (the Author of life!) was putting his own life on the line. He would keep the terms of this agreement or willingly forfeit his life. This should show you how seriously he took the covenant with

Abraham. There was absolutely no question that the Lord was going to do what he promised.

The second amazing thing about this story is that God did *not* require Abraham to walk down between the animal halves. Normally they would both do it; but in this case the Lord knew that Abraham and his descendants would surely put the covenant in jeopardy if it depended on them in any way. So God took upon himself to keep both sides of the bargain. Not that he was allowing Abraham to get away with sin in the future. But he knew that Abraham *would* sin — and since the covenant was tremendously important to the Lord, he was acting now to protect it from any future threats to its fulfillment.

The Terms of the Covenant

What was this covenant that the Lord made with Abraham? There *was* a covenant made before this time with Noah; but Abraham was the first important step in the process of salvation. For a long time the Lord was preparing an answer to the sin and death that man had introduced into his perfect creation. Now, in Abraham, he was ready to start unfolding it into human history. The covenant with Abraham is the beginning of the answer that we have all been looking for.

The Lord promised to do four things for Abraham and his descendants:

> **To give him a son:** Abraham and Sarah had no children when they moved to Canaan in obedience to the Lord's command. They were advanced in years at the time, and had basically given up hope that they ever would have a natural-born son. But the Lord promised them that they would, in fact, have their own son — clearly an impossible thing.

But Abram said, "O Sovereign LORD, what can you give me since I remain childless and the one who will inherit my estate is Eliezer of Damascus?" And Abram said, "You have given me no children; so a servant in my household will be my heir." Then the word of the LORD came to him: "This man will not be your heir, but a son coming from your own body will be your heir." (Genesis 15:2-4)

He was too old to have a son, and his wife was long past the child-bearing age for women. God was promising them the impossible — a miracle, which happens to be the very method he uses to build his kingdom. At one point they both laughed at the idea of having a son in their old age; when the boy was born, then, they named him "Isaac" which means "he laughs" (perhaps because the Lord had the last laugh in this!).

The promise was fulfilled in Genesis 21:

Now the Lord was gracious to Sarah as he had said, and the Lord did for Sarah what he had promised. Sarah became pregnant and bore a son to Abraham in his old age, at the very time God had promised him. (Genesis 21:1-2)

To give him the land: When the Lord brought Abraham to Canaan, it wasn't just for a sight-seeing tour! He had Abraham look around at this new place and promised him that one day, both he and his descendants would own this land.

> Lift up your eyes from where you are and look north and south, east and west. All the land that you see I will give to you and your offspring forever. (Genesis 13:14)

The problem was that this would have to be as much of a miracle as the first promise! The Canaanites who already lived there wouldn't take kindly to an alien with strange ways and accents settling down among them, taking their valuable pasture and resources — they especially wouldn't appreciate his notions of owning the whole place someday! So they no doubt kept their eye on him at all times and encouraged him to move on, not settle down. (You can see this very thing happen in the story of Isaac — Genesis 26:12-31.)

The fulfillment of this promise came about in a strange way, certainly not in the way that Abraham would have wanted. Sarah his wife eventually died, and after Abraham mourned over her he looked around for a place to bury her. Since he had no land of his own, he went to the Hittites (a Canaanite tribe living near Hebron) and asked to buy from them a field with a cave in it so that he could bury her. They agreed on a price and the deed was made out in Abraham's name; he became the legal owner of a piece of Canaanite property for the first time.

> So Ephron's field in Machpelah near Mamre — both the field and the cave in it, and all the trees within the borders of the field — was deeded to Abraham as his property in the presence of all the Hittites who had come to the gate of the city . . . So

the field and the cave in it were deeded to Abraham by the Hittites as a burial site. (Genesis 23:17-18, 20)

The remarkable thing about this transaction was that it was the beginning of the fulfillment of the second promise that God made with Abraham. He was to become owner of the entire land, in spite of the Canaanites already living there. This was the first step to that ownership. It happened in the midst of trial; certainly Abraham didn't want his wife to die. Nevertheless that trial was the means that the Lord used to bring about what otherwise would have never happened. That deed, by the way, stayed in the family until they returned from Egypt hundreds of years later.

To make a great nation from him: The Lord promised Abraham that not only would he get a son, but his descendants would become so numerous that they would be a great nation that nobody could count.

I will make you into a great nation. (Genesis 12:2)

He took him outside and said, "Look up at the heavens and count the stars — if indeed you can count them." Then he said to him, "So shall your offspring be." (Genesis 15:5)

Now Abraham couldn't become a nation all by himself. And his son couldn't become a nation without getting married. So they had a problem on their hands: where to find a wife for Isaac?

Abraham absolutely refused to get one of the local Canaanite girls for Isaac's wife; they were pagans, worshippers of idols and would lead his son into wickedness and away from the Lord. So Abraham had his servant go back home to Haran where his extended family still lived and find a wife there.

Most people use this story as an example of how to find a suitable marriage partner. But we miss the main point of the story if we limit ourselves to just that. Genesis 24 is really showing us the beginning of the fulfillment of the third promise — the making of a nation. He provided a wife (Rebekah) to be the mother of Jacob, who was the father of twelve sons, who were the fathers of the twelve tribes of Israel. The promise had begun to unfold!

> And they blessed Rebekah and said to her, "Our sister, may you increase to thousands upon thousands; may your offspring possess the gates of their enemies." (Genesis 24:60)

To bless the nations through him: When man first sinned in the Garden of Eden, he brought upon himself and the entire world a tremendous curse of misery and death. As far as God was concerned, this was the worst thing that could have happened to his beautiful creation. He didn't curse us because he liked to, but because he had to. He had to confront sin with the severity of the Law because justice is important to him.

But the Lord always did intend to save a few from this disaster. From the very beginning he set about putting together a new answer for the problem of sin and death. He hinted at what it might be in Genesis 3:15, but he didn't really say yet what he had in mind.

Now in Abraham's life he was ready to start putting the plan into action. The first step was to promise Abraham that he would be a blessing to the nations:

And all peoples on earth will be blessed through you. (Genesis 12:3)

And through your offspring all nations on earth will be blessed. (Genesis 22:18)

This blessing would overturn the original curse that fell on mankind. But what would it look like? Again, Abraham got a "foretaste", a glimpse of what that would look like, in his own experience. The Lord told him one time to take his only son Isaac and sacrifice him to the Lord "on one of the mountains I will tell you about." (Genesis 22:2) So Abraham took Isaac there and started to draw the sacrificial knife across his son's throat. Immediately the Lord stopped him and commended him for his faith.

What went through Abraham's mind during this crisis? He was about to lose his only hope! Upon Isaac rested the future of the entire covenant; it didn't make sense to put him to death, even if it *was* in obedience to the Lord. But the Lord showed Abraham a truth there that strengthened him to go on with the act:

Abraham reasoned that God could raise the dead, and figuratively speaking, he did receive Isaac back from death. (Hebrews 11:19)

Abraham learned about resurrection that day; he got the first sample himself when the Lord gave Isaac back to him. This was in fulfillment of the fourth promise — the blessing that God had in mind, eventually, for people all around the world: life from the dead, eternal life.

So in Abraham's own lifetime he saw the beginning of all four of the promises that God had made to him in the covenant. They weren't complete fulfillments; his descendants would see much more as God kept these promises of the covenant. But they were foretastes, glimpses, the first experiences of the reality that God had for him and his children.

The Covenant in Christ

We must move on, however. The Lord had much bigger things in mind for Abraham and his children. Not only was the first taste of the promises insufficient, but all that came after that for many centuries failed to exhaust what God had in mind for Abraham's family. "These were all commended for their faith, yet *none* of them received what had been promised. God had planned something better for us so that only together with us would they be made perfect." (Hebrews 11:39-40)

Imagine a huge mansion, and the front door leads into a small room. From there you can go on into the rest of the mansion and see the richness and vastness of the place, or you can stay there in the little front room and miss out on the rest. Abraham's taste of what God had in mind in the covenant was like that little first room. The covenant was actually referring to the huge spiritual realities that lay beyond the limitations of time and space; it speaks of the Kingdom of God, Heaven, the vast treasuries that lay in God's eternal vaults. The front room is part of the mansion, but it hardly begins to show us what lies beyond its doors.

Abraham himself knew that he was only tasting the first fruits of the Kingdom of God. We have proof of this from the inspired writers of the Bible, who knew for certain (through the Spirit who knows the thoughts and hearts of all men) what went through Abraham's mind during his life. In fact, without this testimony we would never know for sure what Abraham knew! But we *can* know with confidence what Abraham really believed about these things. He knew that their ultimate fulfillment was in Christ.

Let's go through each of the four promises in the covenant and see what Abraham knew then about it or would eventually come to know:

> **The promise of the son:** Abraham knew that his son Isaac wasn't the full promise that God had in mind, when the Lord promised to give him a son. We have proof of this from Jesus himself:
>
> Your father Abraham rejoiced at the thought of seeing *my day*; he saw it and was glad. (John 8:56)
>
> There were several things about the birth of Isaac that taught Abraham what Jesus himself would be like. *First*, Isaac was a miracle baby — his birth was biologically impossible. Sarah was long past her age of bearing children. So was Jesus a miracle baby: he was born with no earthly father, by the action of the Holy Spirit on his mother Mary. *Second*, the covenant that the Lord gave Abraham

was to be passed on to Isaac, not to the other son Ishmael (who was born of the slave woman). Isaac was the rightful heir of all that Abraham owned, including the special promises of the Lord. In the same way, Jesus is the rightful heir of all the promises of God, since he is the only natural Son of God. *Third*, as we shall see in a minute, Isaac's life was all but lost by God's decree, and yet Abraham received him "back from the dead." Jesus actually went through that death (a sacrifice, by the way, like Isaac was supposed to be) and still came back from the dead.

So Abraham knew, in several important ways, what God had in mind for the Son who was to come in the future. How much more he knew about Jesus, we don't know; but we do know, on the testimony of Jesus himself, that he understood the basics of the Christ child. He knew that Jesus was the Heir through which the people of God would receive the blessings given to Abraham.

The promise of the land: Abraham also knew that the dusty piece of real estate called Canaan wasn't all that God had in mind when he promised him and his seed the land. Again, we don't have to guess what was in his mind; we have testimony from someone who was certain about how much Abraham knew about this matter:

> By faith he made his home in the promised land like a stranger in a foreign country; he lived in tents, as did Isaac and Jacob, who were heirs with him of the same promise. For he was looking forward to the

city with foundations, whose architect and builder is God. (Hebrews 11:9-10)

This is another amazing statement, something that we couldn't be sure of unless we had this testimony. Abraham was glad enough to see that his immediate posterity would have a place to live, but the Lord showed him that Canaan itself wasn't good enough for *all* the people of God who would end up coming into the Kingdom. In fact, he himself looked forward to a far better place to live than Palestine, as these verses assure us.

The city that this refers to is the New Jerusalem that the New Testament describes, especially in the book of Revelation. (See Revelation 21-22) Christians don't lay claim to the old Jerusalem like the Jews do; we know that God's Temple is in Heaven, that he lives among his people — the Church — and we are to set our eyes on things above, where Jesus is now, not on things below. (Colossians 3:1-3) This world will one day disappear in judgment, and all of God's faithful servants, including Abraham himself, will live with God in Heaven forever and rule over a new earth.

In fact, Abraham got there ahead of us! Jesus himself assures us that Abraham has gone to his reward — not to the land of Canaan that his earthly descendants inherited from him, but the land of glory that God originally planned to give him. You can see this testimony in the story about Lazarus and the rich man. (Luke 16:19-31)

The promise of the nation: Abraham saw the beginning of the promise of a great nation when he got his son Isaac a wife and they started their family. Whether he knew at the time what would come of this marriage, we don't know; we do know that Abraham knows *now* what came of it! Obviously, as we see in the story of Lazarus (Luke 16), after Abraham died he evidently went to be with God. Shortly after arriving, he started receiving visitors — his own "children," in fact! As each new generation of Jews came and went in Canaan, some of them at least went on to glory to join Abraham there in Heaven. But don't miss the significance of who these people are: they are heirs of the promise of Heaven, just as Abraham was, because they are *children* of Abraham.

We don't know how many people there are in Heaven now, but we do know that the number is growing. Lazarus obviously is one of them. But look again at the testimony of Jesus, who came from Heaven and is an eyewitness of what is going on there right now:

> I say to you that many will come from the east and the west, and will take their places at the feast with Abraham, Isaac and Jacob in the kingdom of Heaven. (Matthew 8:11)

The family of Abraham is getting larger, and they are gathering in Heaven for the great feast that God has planned for them. Perhaps Abraham was surprised to see *so many* Gentiles there, and *so few* of the Jews there! "But the subjects of the kingdom will be thrown outside, into the darkness, where there will be weeping and gnashing of teeth." (Matthew 8:12) At any rate he knows now exactly what God had in mind when he promised that he would become the father of a great nation.

The nation, of course, is the Church of God — the body of Christ, which consists of all believers whether they are Jew or Gentile. There used to be strict regulations about letting Gentiles around holy things, especially the Temple. But in Christ the barrier was broken down and the two parties were made one body, one believing Church. (Ephesians 2:11-22) Not everyone who was born a Jew became part of the Church, which shows that God never had *only* the physical family of Abraham in mind when he made that promise at the beginning. Rather, only those who had the faith of Abraham – Jew or Gentile – would be a part of the family of God.

The promise of the blessing: When Abraham came so close to sacrificing his son Isaac, he thought that death was certain. But he also knew that God wouldn't leave it that way. We already saw the testimony of Hebrews about this:

> Abraham reasoned that God could raise the dead, and figuratively speaking, he did receive Isaac back from death. (Hebrews 11:19)

In other words, he learned something about God and his ways: the Lord intends to raise his promised children from the dead. Death will not be the end of us; we will live again, never to die again, to serve the Lord forever.

How much Abraham really knew about the resurrection that God has in mind for the Church of Christ, we don't know. Perhaps he didn't know the many details that we have now in the Scriptures —

like the teachings of Thessalonians and 1 Corinthians 15. But he did understand the concept, and he knew the mind of the Lord about the matter. As far as God is concerned, death is *not* the last word over us: Abraham knew this for certain about his own son. There was just too much hanging in the balance, too much to happen in the coming kingdom, to let death be the end.

The resurrection is the great hope of the Church, and it's a hope that the unbelievers don't have. Nobody but Abraham and his children have the right to expect that God will raise them out of the grave into newness of life and give them eternity in Heaven. It's a special promise to the family of Abraham; it's going to overturn everything that sin and death has done to ruin us. The resurrection will be much more than just a physical reversal, however; it will be a new kind of life — as Paul carefully explains in 1 Corinthians 15. This life will defeat death forever; it will be a life with God, never to fall into sin or darkness again.

The Gospel

Now these promises are things that every Christian knows about and hopes for. What we may not have known, however, is that they were originally given to Abraham long ago! They aren't our property but his property. We have them only by inheritance; he had them given to him directly by God. Abraham has the signed covenant in his hand, so to speak; that's his hope. We, however, have to prove that we are actually his children if we want to share in his property.

Let's look at this another way. What could you possibly be hoping to get from God except these four things? Isn't **Christ** the very one you love the most, your only Friend and Savior, your "all in all," your source to the treasures of Heaven? Isn't **Heaven** your hope, the place that Jesus went to prepare for your coming, your only home? Isn't the **Church** your new family, the ones who care about your spiritual state and who minister to your spiritual needs? Isn't the **resurrection** going to be the end of all that is bad in this world and the start of an eternity of bliss and joy and holiness? What more could you want but these things? What else did you hear about in the Gospel and put your hope in?

My point is that *this is* your faith; there isn't anything else important that you could want from God but these promises. So if these are what you want and expect because of your faith, you are wanting the *covenant promises* that the Lord gave Abraham long ago! These spiritual realities, as fully as you know them now, were what Abraham received from God's hand. And if you want Abraham's property, you must prove your relationship to him in order to legally get it. Only Abraham's heirs will get the promises of God.

The Law

So then, the law is holy, and the commandment is holy, righteous and good.
(Romans 7:12)

The Law is confusing to Christians. For one thing, it's part of our Bible – and the Prophets and Christ and the Apostles had a high regard for the Law. But on the other hand, the New Testament appears to warn us away from keeping the Law; Paul goes to great lengths in the book of Galatians to convince us that there's no hope in keeping the Law, even for Spirit-filled Christians. So what are we to do with the Law? Keep all of it? Or only some of it? Or should we just ignore it?

First let's define what exactly the Law is. The **Law** (Hebrew "Torah" – תּוֹרָה) is technically the 613 Laws that were given to Israel at Mt. Sinai through Moses. They are found in the first five books of the Bible: Genesis, Exodus, Leviticus, Numbers, & Deuteronomy – the books which themselves are also called "the Torah." All the rest of the Bible writers understood that this is the Law in the Bible. The Prophets expand and interpret the Law, David praises the Law, Jesus fulfilled this Law, the Apostles looked for the fulfillment of the Law through the work of the Spirit. Some people try to call the entire Bible "the Law of God," but this is inaccurate and misleading.

The Law condemns sinners

One great purpose of the Law is this: to condemn mankind. Paul tells us in Romans what the Law does to us:

Indeed I would not have known what sin was except through the Law. For I would not have known what coveting really was if the Law had not said, "Do not covet." (Romans 7:7)

The Law tells us exactly what sin is. We need that, because until the Law came, people didn't exactly know what offended God about human behavior. They made up their own definitions of what is right and wrong, and as a result there were as many systems of morality and ethics as there were men and nations! What was "right" in one culture, was "wrong" in another. People were confused about the true nature of sin.

So, God gave the Law in order to clear up the confusion. "Here is what sin is," he told us. And with that definition of sin, he condemned every human being who has ever lived, because nobody has ever kept *this* Law perfectly. We are all guilty of breaking God's Law in some way, during some time in our lives. Even such a simple version of the Law as the Ten Commandments is enough to prove every one of us a sinner. The Law isn't trying to make us friends with God; it is proving, without a shadow of a doubt, that we are already his enemies.

Keep in mind that the Law has a double edge. Not only does it define what sin is, it also demands a penalty for anybody who commits sin: punishment. The Law is no friend! If we fulfill the Law in every way, it will leave us alone. But if we offend God in even one matter, it rises up in wrath and condemns us.

So then, the Law is holy, and the commandment is holy, righteous and good. Did that which is good, then, become death to me? By no means! But in order that sin might be recognized as sin, it produced death in me through what was good, so that through the commandment sin might become utterly sinful. (Romans 7:12-13)

Why some people feel so comfortable living in the shadow of the Law, I will never understand. They don't know that they live under the shadow of *death*. The Law means trouble for sinners; going to the Law for help or comfort is like reaching out to pet a guard dog that is trained to kill strangers.

The Law hurts. The only way that it wouldn't hurt anybody is if that person kept the whole Law, perfectly, all his life. With such a person the Law has no argument or problem. But if it finds the least blemish in him, the smallest offense, then the Law becomes a fierce enemy. That sin has challenged the glory of God, and the Law will not rest until there is blood shed. "In fact, the Law requires that nearly everything be cleansed with blood, and without the shedding of blood there is no forgiveness." (Hebrews 9:22)

Picking and Choosing

A *legalist* is someone who finds it necessary to obey the letter of the Law. This means that they read the Law in the Old Testament and feel that they must obey exactly what it says. They also try to make others feel that same obligation.

Legalists tell us that all of us must obey the Law in some way; we may not have to obey *all* of the Law, they tell us, but at least the more important parts of it. They teach that the Ten Commandments are essential for every Christian. Some of the more extreme legalists even pick out other parts of the Law and try to obligate Christians to live by those too — for example, the Sabbath laws, and the laws concerning food, and the "clean and unclean" laws. Some legalists pick out the "ceremonial" laws that they feel we should use in church, and the "civil" laws that modern societies should use.

The biggest problem about legalists is this: they pick and choose the laws that they say we must obey. The reason that they are so choosy (which they usually won't be honest enough to tell you!) is that, when you read the Law of Moses, it becomes obvious to you that *nobody* can keep all those laws. Even if we wanted to, it would be impossible in our modern society to obey everything that the Old Testament Law demands. Even the legalists will admit this!

However, you can't pick and choose the laws that you want to obey. They are all one body of Law; it was God's Word given through Moses, all of it, and as the Scripture says, "Whoever keeps the whole Law and yet stumbles at just one point is guilty of breaking all of it." (James 2:10) When once you have set your hand to keeping the Law, you are obligated to keep *all* of it. "Cursed is everyone who does not continue to do *everything* written in the Book of the Law." (Galatians 3:10) The Lord will not be impressed with your arguments that you thought you only had to keep part of it; that's not what *he* said to do with it!

There are important reasons why you can't pick and choose the laws that you want to obey and ignore the rest. ***First***, there is the fact that these laws are all part of the great body of Law that the Lord gave the Israelites through Moses. It was all given to Israel, as the rules of the Kingdom of God, and none of them were given to other nations. It was the way the nation was to operate, the government over God's people. The Israelites were bound to keep the *whole* Law, not just the parts that they liked best. Now if any of those laws are still binding today, then they all are, since it's all the Law of God. There is nothing in Scripture which says that parts of the Law are still in effect while others are no longer in effect. And you certainly don't have the freedom to decide how you are going to obey the Law. If Congress passes a law that says you owe them a certain percentage of your income in taxes, you are not free to send them a truckload of apples in payment of the tax! If you don't do exactly what the law says, you are considered a law breaker, no matter what your intentions are. The same is true of God's Law.

Second, the laws are tied together inextricably. If you decide that you want to follow a particular law, you will have to decide what you are going to do about some of the other laws as well, because they tie into the one that you are looking at. For example, some modern groups teach that we must follow the food regulations that are given in the Law. Some foods were "unclean" to the Israelites and they weren't allowed to eat them. The problem was that this wasn't only a health issue, it was a ceremonial issue as well. Anybody who even touched one of these forbidden animals was unclean and had to undergo ceremonial washings and stay away from other people for an appointed time. Any pots that touched this food had to be destroyed. And this wasn't a small matter to God:

> Do not defile yourselves by any of these creatures. Do not make yourselves unclean by means of them or be made unclean by them. I am the Lord your God; consecrate yourselves and be holy, because I am holy. Do not make yourselves unclean by any creature that moves about on the ground. I am the Lord who brought you up out of Egypt to be your God; therefore be holy, because I am holy. (Leviticus 11:43-45)

When the Lord said something like this, you can be sure that he meant what he said — all of it — and you had better do *exactly* what he said. The problem is that if we were to take this seriously today, we may as well resign ourselves to being perpetual lawbreakers because none of us can do all that this law requires. Not only are we not capable of doing *our* part, but the society we live in isn't going to do its part either — which means that we are being polluted against our will! The point here is that once you decide to follow any particular law, you are immediately going to run into trouble with other laws that are tied into it. And you can't get out of the dilemma by saying, "Well, I must do the right thing even if others don't." According to the Law, what others do will make *you* unclean and affect *your* relationship with God.

Third, the Law not only consists of commands about how to live life, it also makes provision for enforcing those laws — the priesthood and the Temple. The priests were the enforcers of the Law, much as policemen are enforcers of the laws of our society. They didn't perform the Law for the people; the people themselves had to follow the Law's commands and report to the priests with the results. And many of the laws had to do with the daily and special functions that went on in the Temple. None of that is in operation today; even if we wanted to follow some of the laws, there is no way we can follow through with them and complete the requirements of satisfying the priest and offering sacrifices in the Temple. All that is gone now. Even the Jews understand this problem. Their system right now is almost useless to them; they are waiting for the day when they can rebuild the Temple and put the whole system back in place. Then keeping one particular law will be meaningful because all the other related laws will be there to support it.

Once you see the problem here, you will be more willing to start looking elsewhere for your personal righteousness. There is no hope that you or anybody else on earth can keep those 613 Laws to the perfection that God demands!

Christ and the Law

Christ stands in a unique position in regard to the Law of God. He alone was able to fulfill the Law perfectly; the Law has no complaint about the character and actions of Jesus Christ. This is an amazing record, in light of how complex and demanding the Law is. But it's also understandable, since Jesus is the Son of God and could do no other than keep his own Law to the letter!

Christ related to the Law on several levels; in order to understand our own relationship with the Law, we have to distinguish each of the things that Jesus did for us:

- **_What he did with the Law:_** Christ came to earth to do more than keep the Law for his own sake. He came to solve man's problem of sin, which is *lawlessness*. The Law's complaint is with us, not with him. So here is what Jesus did: he became man, like us except for our sin, so that he could be "under the Law" and accomplish his goal. Then *as man* he fulfilled the Law completely and perfectly. When he was done, the Law was forced to admit that *a man* had kept the Law to God's satisfaction! This was the first time that such a thing had happened. Even though the Israelites had the Law for almost 1500 years, nobody had ever kept it perfectly until Jesus came.

- **_What he did for us:_** Now for the final step in God's plan of salvation. Jesus sent his Spirit and made us *one with him* — we are in him, united to him in all ways, so that whatever happens to him will also happen to us. This means several things: *first*, since the Law is satisfied with him, it is also satisfied with us. There is nothing more to be done! This is what Hebrews means when it says that we *rest* in Christ; he rested from his labors (remember his last words on the cross? "It is finished." John 19:30) and now we rest in him. "Take my yoke upon you and learn from me, for I am gentle and humble in heart, and you will find rest for your souls." (Matthew 11:29) The work of satisfying the Law is over now, for him *and* for us. If there were any more to do on this score then salvation wouldn't be done yet!

Second, whatever rewards are in store for Christ as the perfect man, we also can expect to receive. If he was lifted on high, we will be too. (Colossians 3:1) If he sits at God's right hand, so will we. (Colossians 3:3) If he will rule over the universe, so will we. (Colossians 3:4) Since we are one with him, we will share in his glory and receive the inheritance that Jesus bought for us.

Everything that happens *to us* must go *through him* first; he put himself between us and the Law for this reason. And since he did this, we never deal with the Law directly. There is no salvation in that! Our only hope is in what Christ, as the firstborn of many brethren, achieved for us and passes on to us.

Since Christ fulfilled the Law for us, what is left for us to do? Can we sin now and not have to worry about punishment since Christ took that burden upon himself? Paul tells us that such a thing is unthinkable! "By no means! We died to sin; how can we live in it any longer?" (Romans 6:2) Remember why Jesus came: he came to save us *from* our sin, not leave us in it. "You are to give him the name Jesus, because *he will save his people from their sins.*" (Matthew 1:21)

- ***What he does in us:*** He died to save us from condemnation, but that's only one thing he wanted to do. The other was to get us out of the moral mess that resulted in our condemnation in the first place.

So, right now the Lord Jesus is busy with our sanctification — the process of making us holy and set apart for the Lord's use. He is applying *his* righteousness to *our* souls so that we look more and more like him. "And so he condemned sin in sinful man, in order that *the righteous requirements of the Law might be fully met in us*, who do not live according to the sinful nature but according to the Spirit." (Romans 8:3-4) Did you catch that phrase about the Law? The Law of God hasn't gone away; it wasn't put away permanently when Jesus fulfilled it. The Law isn't going away because the God whom it describes isn't going away. Jesus is *making* us conform to what the Law says is a righteous man; only he can do that, of course, since only he lived that righteous life. But the fact remains that the Law is still in full force; the only difference now is *who* has to keep the Law. If we do it, the outcome is in serious question; if Christ does it, it is certain to succeed.

There is a prophecy in Ezekiel that shows us what God had in mind long before Jesus came to earth, but is exactly in line with what the New Testament teaches about our present relationship with the Law.

> I will give you a new heart and put a new spirit in you; I will remove from you your heart of stone and give you a heart of flesh. And I will put my Spirit in you and *move you* to follow my decrees and be careful to keep my laws. (Ezekiel 36:26-27)

This agrees with what Paul says about the subject. The Lord will put his Spirit into us, and the Spirit will make us conform to the requirements of the Law. Before this time the Israelites were doing their best to obey the Law — and failing at it. It just couldn't be done by sinners. God finally got tired of fooling with them and predicted the time when *he* would make them righteous; instead of waiting on them to do what is right, he would change their hearts himself. When this happens, of course, he will get the credit for the job, because if the Spirit is making you conform to the requirements of the Law then *you* can't claim any credit for doing it! But that's what being part of the Church is all about; it's an entirely different thing from what the Israelites were living under.

- **_What he's doing right now:_** Christ is also doing something *right now* in respect to the Law. He fulfilled its requirements as far as living a righteous life; but he is also in the Heavenly Temple right now fulfilling his duties as our High Priest. The earthly Temple was a picture of the one in Heaven: if you want to know what it's like in God's eternal Temple, read the description in the Law of the Israelite Temple. You must realize, however, that none of that has disappeared from Heaven as the earthly one has. Though the Jews lost their Temple, God still lives in his! And there must still be a sacrifice on the altar to atone for the people's sins — but now it's Jesus' eternal sacrifice that was made "once for all" for our sake. (Hebrews 12:24) There must still be incense burning day and night — though in God's Temple that is the "prayers of the saints" that always go up to him. (Revelation 5:8) There must still be a Holy of Holies, because that's where God sits and rules over his people and gives them what they come to him and ask for. Now, however, the veil that used to separate us from God is torn away and the way into the Holy of Holies is open to "whosoever will." (Hebrews 10:19-22) And the High Priest still lives to intercede for the people:

Christ is always presenting our requests to the Father and getting answers for us. (Romans 8:34)

So the Law hasn't gone anywhere. It's still in full force, because that is still the way that God wants to run his kingdom. The difference now is that Jesus is doing all these legal requirements for us and sending us the benefits.

The Christian and the Law

If you really want to do what the Law says — if you feel obligated to keep the Law in any way at all — there is nothing wrong with that. Christ did that very thing! If it was wrong to even try, then he would have been wrong for doing it. The problem is that *you would be a fool to try to keep the Law in any way at all.* The Law condemns sinners; that is its purpose. If you try to obey the Law and fail in any way at all, you are condemned as a law breaker and must be punished. When you start down that direction, you must do everything perfectly and not make a single slip or you have failed. And a sinner doesn't have the liberty to try again; there is only punishment in store for him, not mercy, when it comes to the Law.

> I would like to learn just one thing from you: Did you receive the Spirit by observing the Law, or by believing what you heard? Are you so foolish? After beginning with the Spirit, are you now trying to attain your goal by human effort? Have you suffered so much for nothing — if it really was for nothing? Does God give you his Spirit and work miracles among you because you observe the Law, or because you believe what you heard? (Galatians 3:2-5)

One reason we get confused about our relationship with the Law is because we are continually enjoying the benefits of God's grace even while we struggle unsuccessfully with the Law. What I mean is this: we decide to struggle with our sin by obeying the Law; then we fail, since sinful flesh can't keep the Law to God's strict requirements; then we go to God for breaking the Law and are restored to fellowship with him; then we try the Law again. We often misinterpret the spiritual success that comes by walking in faith, thinking that our success came as a result of our attempts at walking according to the Law. We need to get it straight in our minds that any spiritual success we may have comes from the mercy of God in Christ, and Christ living in us through his Spirit, not by our pitiful efforts at keeping the Law.

Don't underestimate the power of the Law. It looks simple enough, as if you could successfully keep it if you tried hard enough. But better men than you have tried it and failed. Remember the rich young ruler who boasted that, as concerns the Law, "all these I have kept." (Matthew 19:20) Yet he did not have eternal life because his best efforts at Law-keeping weren't good enough for Christ. There is a spiritual depth to the Law that is truly frightening, and an honest soul knows better than to take on such work alone. It's far better to let Christ do it for us.

The question often arises – what about the Ten Commandments? Aren't even Christians obligated to follow that great Law? But if you've been following the argument so far, you will know two things already: ***first***, you can't obey the Ten Commandments either, not to the extent that God expects of you. Don't make the mistake that the rich young ruler made, thinking that a superficial obedience to this simple list will make you pleasing to God. Read about the true, spiritual depth of this Law in the Sermon on the Mount (Matthew 5-7) and then honestly answer whether you can do that without anybody's help!

Second, Jesus fulfilled these commands for you, and by means of his Spirit he intends to change your heart so that you will look like what the Ten Commandments expect. But the *way* to that righteousness is unexpected: it's not by tackling the Commandments directly! Jesus gave us a clue on this:

> And I will ask the Father, and he will give you another Counselor to be with you forever – the Spirit of truth. The world cannot accept him, because it neither sees him nor knows him. But you know him, for he lives with you and will be in you. (John 14:16-17)

Now we reach our goal of righteousness not by obeying the Law, but by walking in the Spirit of God – the Spirit that Jesus sent us from Heaven to make us one with him. Remember that love (which the Law demands of us) is one of the fruit of the Spirit. There is our salvation; and there is God's solution for our problem of sin.

Should we even study the Law then? By all means, *yes!* The Law has a lot to do with you. *First*, the Law describes what is wrong with you, the reasons that God sent a Savior to save you. If we didn't have the Law we wouldn't understand the true nature of sin and would never know the real need for a Savior. *Second*, the Law perfectly describes Christ. Jesus is what you were never able to become on your own. If for no other reason, you need to know the Law so that you can praise your Lord for being so perfect. *Third*, Jesus kept the Law for your sake. These requirements are still in full force, even today. God still will not accept anybody into his Kingdom who doesn't conform to the strict requirements of the Law. We shouldn't be little children in our thinking. We should know what Christ has done for us, we should know our new standing with God and how it was possible. We should also know what Christ is doing on our behalf now — he is still fulfilling the Law's requirements before the Throne of Grace in the Temple in Heaven. All this, which is described completely in the Law, has a lot to do with our faith in Christ.

Finally, the end result is the same. The man who perfectly fulfills the Law is considered a "righteous man" in the sight of God. Only Christ has done this, however. And for the man who has faith in Christ, the Spirit will put Christ's righteousness into his life too, so that through his walk of faith, hope and love he will fulfill the righteous requirements of the Law. "Therefore love is the fulfillment of the Law." (Romans 13:10) In other words, as we follow the Lord in the Spirit, the Law is satisfied. This is a mystery, but the end result – righteousness – is the same. The difference is in *how* you go about it.

The Promised Land

For the LORD your God is bringing you into a good land.
(Deuteronomy 8:7)

When the Israelites were led out of slavery in Egypt, they were promised a land of their own – a "land flowing with milk and honey." (Exodus 3:8) God's intention was to form them into his own nation, his own people, and take them to Palestine where he and they would live together in joy and righteousness forever.

This is the first great story of deliverance in the Bible – out of Egypt, across the Red Sea, through the wilderness, and finally to Canaan and rest. It was literally the birth of Israel; and it serves as the model of how God delivers all of his people – including us Christians. Our Savior delivers us from bondage, no hope, and death into freedom, inheritance, and eternal life.

Joshua and Jesus

The Hebrew name Joshua (יְהוֹשֻׁעַ) is actually the same name that Jesus had.

Greek		**Hebrew**
Jesus (Ἰησοῦς)	⬅———	Joshua (יְהוֹשֻׁעַ)

"Jesus" is the Greek form of *Yehoshua*, or Joshua. So if Jesus would have lived in Old Testament times, he would have been called Joshua; and if Joshua had lived in New Testament times he would have been called Jesus.

The name **Yehoshua** is a combination of two words –

"Yah" (short for **Yahweh**, or יהוה), and ...

"yasha" (ישע) which means "to save"

So both "Jesus" and "Joshua" mean "Yahweh saves." Thus this name was given to the two great deliverers and conquerors of the Bible, Old and New Testaments.

The identical names weren't an accident. Both Joshua and Jesus led the people of God into the Promised Land. Joshua's job, in fact, was not only to subdue Canaan and divide out the inheritance among the tribes of Israel, but to teach us on a spiritual level what Jesus would later do for *his* people. Remember that the purpose of the Old Testament stories is to slow the process down and teach us who *Jesus* is. In the story of Joshua taking Canaan, we can easily see the separate parts of the Conquest. So now we know, from reading this account, what the separate parts are in the parallel work of Christ. If we didn't first have the account of Joshua where everything is laid out so clearly, we certainly would have had a more difficult time picking out those same truths in the complex stories of the Gospels!

Also keep in mind that the Old Testament characters who teach us about Christ are usually only wearing one hat, so to speak. Joshua symbolizes *one* aspect of Christ in his particular work. There are many other dimensions to the ministry of Christ than just what we learn in Joshua's work – for example, Moses showed us the aspect of Jesus being a Prophet and Law-giver; Joseph illustrates the Son at God's right hand, protecting his people from death; David used five principles to build up Israel that Jesus later uses on his Church. We therefore can't take any particular Old Testament individual and push the parallels too far.

Through the life of each person, God shows us a little bit of the massive work that Christ did in himself. This too should make us appreciate how much this one man Jesus did for us! It took Joshua, and Moses, and David, and Joseph, and Abraham, and scores of others in the Old Testament to fully describe the work of Christ for us. Only by putting it all together do we get a more complete picture of who Jesus is.

- **Joshua led God's people into the Promised Land.** This was a big step, one that the descendants of Abraham had been looking forward to for hundreds of years. The promise of the land of Canaan was part of the covenant made between the Lord and their father Abraham in 2000 BC – and now 600 years later the Israelites were going to collect on that promise.

    The first step of making Israel into a nation was accomplished at Mt. Sinai. But it wasn't enough that the Lord called the people to himself. He wanted to bless them richly – he wanted to give them a home of their own, fields for food and homes to raise their families in peace. He wanted to gather them together around his throne in a land "flowing with milk and honey." His idea was to create a safe haven (much like the Garden of Eden was for Adam and Eve) where he would live with his people and they would live with him. Ideally they would be the central spot of earth – through the Israelites the Lord would come to rule all the nations of the earth.

    Jesus is also gathering his people together to bless them richly. It's not enough for him to save them from their sins; he wants to lead them to their own home, their own land where they can live in "peace and righteousness." He told his disciples that he "was going to prepare a place" (John 14:2-3), where "the dwelling of God is with men." (Revelation 21:3) That's why the Scriptures say that this world we live in now is not our home; we are aliens while we live here, wandering through life until the Lord leads us into the eternal Promised Land. (1 Peter 2:11)

Yet we are already tasting the fruits of that new land that we've been promised. While we may be aliens in this world, we have already "entered into the rest" (Hebrews 4:1-11) through Christ's work of redemption; we are *right now* citizens of God's Kingdom. "Consequently, you are no longer foreigners and aliens, but fellow citizens with God's people and members of God's household." (Ephesians 2:19) And with Christ, we will reign over the entire universe from his throne in Heaven.

- **Joshua eliminated the enemy.** His orders were to kill every human being in the land of Canaan. That sounds harsh, but we have to remember who is giving the orders here. The Lord owns all creatures and by rights can dispense with any of them as he wishes. When he told Joshua to kill all the Canaanites, he had good reasons for doing so.

  The Canaanites were immoral wretches; they were known for their immorality all over the Middle East. Remember that Sodom and Gomorrah were on the outer fringes of the territory, and the Lord made them an example of how he punishes reprobates. What made things worse was that the Canaanites worshipped gods that brought out the worst in people – for example, gods that expected religious prostitution, and gods that demanded children sacrificed in fire.

  Having mercy on such people wouldn't solve the problem; they would only go back to their sin and ignore the Lord's warnings to them. God knew that their hearts were hardened in wickedness and they would never repent. In fact, letting them live would only prove to be disastrous to the Israelites themselves because the Canaanites would take acts of mercy for granted and try to tempt God's people into their sins. No, there was only one solution – to eliminate them all. Then the Israelites could focus on the true God and live a holy life before him.

Though man might think that he can get away with his sin – he can even pass laws to protect himself, so that he can commit immorality or at least get off easily if he's caught – none of that passes God's bar of judgment. Immorality and wickedness violate the covenant that God made with mankind at Creation. No matter what kinds of laws we might pass to protect our "rights" nowadays, the Lord expects only one thing from us: *obedience to him and his Law*. We are his servants; we were created to serve him alone. If we don't do that, our lives are forfeit. The King will dispose of us as worthless and rebellious traitors to the state.

Someday people will wake up to that real dimension in God's Kingdom. Jesus himself will come back to work vengeance on God's enemies, and when he does he won't be the humble servant that he was the first time he came. He will come in power, in the wrath of God, wrapped in glory and followed by the hosts of Heaven. The book of Revelation is a clear picture of what Christ will be like when he comes back to earth to do battle with his enemies.

The primary enemy he intends to destroy is the devil. (1 John 3:8) The devil has been working from the beginning of the world to destroy God's works, and therefore Jesus must lay the ax to the root of that tree and destroy it. Take the devil out of the picture, and the Lord has eliminated a major source of temptation, rebellion and wickedness for mankind. So he will have no mercy on his enemy: the devil *will* be destroyed in eternal fire for the crime of perverting God's creation. (Matthew 25:41; Revelation 20:10)

The terrible reality is that he also fully intends to destroy all those who have taken up the devil's cause. On Judgment Day there will be no mercy for the wicked: they will discover too late that the day of salvation was in *this* life, not in the next one.

- **Joshua cleaned the sin out of Canaan.** The Canaanites were known to be immoral wretches, even in those times when immorality was the rule of life. In fact, they had been cooking up disaster for themselves for hundreds of years. In Genesis 15:16 we read God telling Abraham that the pagans in that area weren't yet to the point of destruction – "In the fourth generation your descendants will come back here, for the sin of the Amorites has not yet reached its full measure." In other words, he had his eye on these people and he wasn't going to let them get away with their sin. Judgment would eventually come.

In getting rid of the Canaanites Joshua was also eliminating the sin they were known for. God hates the sin they wallow in and what they've made of themselves by it. People often quote John 3:16 wrongly, as if God will have mercy on *everyone* and forgive them of their sin. But they don't understand God's justice. He who sins will die; that's the Law. It's true that God hates sin and not the creature that he himself formed in his image; but when man refuses to repent and continues in that sin, he has himself ruined the image that God first put in his heart. There's nothing there to love when the image in man's heart is a picture of the devil! So there will be a lot of sinners in Hell who thought God wouldn't do such a thing to them.

The idea was to get the temptation to sin out of the physical area. If the Canaanites wouldn't part with their sin (and God knew they wouldn't) then the job was to get rid of the Canaanites. God does not want his people to be even exposed to sin, let alone play with it. Sin is destructive; it's treason against God and his Kingdom; it's a slap in the Creator's face; it's poison and death to whoever touches it.

This is the very thing that Jesus has come to do for his people. His name – Jesus (which means "Yahweh saves") was deliberately given to him because "he will save his people from their sin." (Matthew 1:21) He's not only going to *forgive* them of their sin – a necessary act to keep them out of reach of the condemnation of the Law – but he will *save* them from the power of sin. That curse must be broken, because he doesn't want his people to keep buckling under the pressure of temptation.

Sin is the primary problem of the human race. We might not think much of it, but to God it's the one curse that must be dealt with. He can think of nothing else while we're still on this earth! So Jesus will take whatever measures are necessary to root the problem out of our hearts and lives. For example, he puts the Holy Spirit in the hearts of all of his believers for the purpose of cleaning up their lives in preparation for living in Heaven.

- **Joshua assigned everyone a portion of the inheritance.** Each tribe was to get a part of the land, extending from Dan in the north to Beersheba in the south. You can see by the map below that they were all taken care of. The boundaries were clear; everyone got land, even Zelophehad's daughters! When one of the tribes complained that they didn't get enough land for all their population, Joshua gave them a section somewhere else to take care of their needs. The idea was that the Lord intended to bless his people and therefore everyone was going to get what they needed. Everyone would have to admit in the end that the Lord was more than gracious to them.

Also note that the land was called an "inheritance," because it was the fulfillment of the covenant that the Lord made with Abraham. Abraham received a rich treasure from the Lord in this covenant, and it was a precious thing that was passed down through the family from son to son. Being a legal agreement, the descendants of Abraham could each lay claim to part of the title. Whatever the Lord promised to do for Abraham, in other words, the children of Abraham also looked forward to as their right and privilege. Not that they *deserved* any of it, but it showed how faithful the Lord is to his promises. God was under obligation by his own oath to bless his people.

This is the same picture that we have in Christ. He bought with his own blood the treasures of Heaven. Being his, he can dispose of them as he wishes – and his wish is that the spiritual children of Abraham share in the inheritance. He made us heirs of God – we who formerly had no legal claim on the riches of Heaven – who can now expect a part of the Promised Land as our very own. He gives "gifts to men" (Ephesians 4:8) as he wishes; he bestows spiritual gifts (Ephesians 4:11-12), he gives the Holy Spirit (Ephesians 1:13-14), he gives a foretaste of the riches to come, he makes promises to his followers of thrones and ruling in eternity. (Matthew 19:28-29) All this is, by law, his to give away. And what we receive is what only a son and heir would receive. Even angels long to look into the amazing transactions that are going on in God's Kingdom – human beings (redeemed, of course) being promised thrones and crowns in Heaven with Christ the Son and heir of God!

- **Joshua gave them homes and lands.** The Lord had promised to give the Israelites the land of Canaan, but along with that promise came a special boon: the Canaanites' fields and homes were included in the deal. They would find, when they took over the land, everything already set up, built, planted, and waiting for them to enjoy.

> When the LORD your God brings you into the land he swore to your fathers, to Abraham, Isaac and Jacob, to give you – a land with large, flourishing cities you did not build, houses filled with all kinds of good things you did not provide, wells you did not dig, and vineyards and olive groves you did not plant – then when you eat and are satisfied, be careful that you do not forget the LORD, who brought you out of Egypt, out of the land of slavery. (Deuteronomy 6:10-12)

This too shows the love and compassion that God has for his people. They wouldn't always have time, right after the wars with the Canaanites, to build a house for their families, or plow and plant fields to get food for their families. God was looking out for them in every detail.

In the Kingdom that Jesus is leading his people into, they will find all the amenities of life waiting for them too. Jesus said that he's going to prepare a place in his Father's house for all of his followers, and then come back to take us there when his work is done.

> In my Father's house are many rooms; if it were not so, I would have told you. I am going there to prepare a place for you. And if I go and prepare a place for you, I will come back and take you to be with me that you also may be where I am. (John 14:2-3)

They will find everything they need in God's house – for example, God himself will be their light. (Revelation 21:23; 22:5) They will eat from fruit trees that bear all year long, and drink from a river that flows forever from God's throne. (Revelation 22:1-2) They will sit down at a feast prepared for them (Matthew 8:11), and they will lack nothing that they need – because God himself will be the source of all good things for them.

We wonder in this life whether Heaven will really replace this world, whether we are foolishly giving up valuable things here in order to chase after spiritual promises that we can't see. But Jesus assured his disciples that "everyone who has left houses or brothers or sisters or father or mother or children or fields for my sake will receive a hundred times as much and will inherit eternal life." (Matthew 19:29) We needn't worry about whether Heaven will be worth the wait or the sacrifices that we're making here; Jesus intends to bless us beyond our wildest imaginations. (Ephesians 3:20)

- **Joshua's work involved miracles.** From the very first public act of Joshua – the miraculous crossing of the Jordan River – it was plain that the Lord's hand was involved in Joshua's ministry. Only God could have done the wonders that occurred during the conquest.

    Jericho was the second example of what God could and would do through his servant. The fiasco at Ai only supported that idea: when someone in the camp deliberately disobeyed orders, the Lord refused to help the Israelites and they lost the battle. When they straightened out the problem, he went back to helping them with the power of Heaven.

    This shows us something important about God and his Kingdom: he uses miracles to build it, because there are certain things that God's people need that only miracles can fulfill. Jericho, for example, was an exceptionally strong city and, the story tells us, "Now Jericho was tightly shut up because of the Israelites. No one went out and no one came in." (Joshua 6:1) It would be pretty much impossible for the Israelites to take the city without a long siege and a lot of bloodshed and trouble. So the Lord demolished the city on the spot for them, so that they could go on into the rest of Canaan and get busy with their work.

    Jesus also works miracles at the points of crisis in our lives for the same reasons. There are certain things we are called to do, but to get started in that direction would require solving some enormous problems that we can't handle on our own. For example, we have been called to be holy. But that's impossible for a human being to do, considering how steeped in sin our hearts are. So to break down the obstacles, Jesus does a miracle and changes our hearts from stone to flesh (Ezekiel 36:26), and fills us with his Holy Spirit who will guide us into truth and righteousness. Suddenly the road that used to be full of boulders and obstacles is cleared off and we can go on.

When the Israelites were about to cross the Jordan River they had to trust God to do the impossible and dry up the river upstream. In fact, they had to put their feet in the water first, *before* God would do that for them! Doesn't Jesus expect the same from us? He gave us impossible jobs to do – to follow the Spirit wherever he leads us, to do battle against the enemy, pray in such a way that we come into God's presence, to love our neighbor. These and many more responsibilities all require a miracle from Jesus first before we can even get started on them. But we will need more miracles as well, because the world is full of problems and the enemy isn't going to accept defeat for long. Our only hope is that the Lord will always be there at our side, as he promised (Matthew 28:20), clearing the way for us to make our work possible.

- **The people themselves had to fight.** Though the Lord promised to give the land to the Israelites, Joshua wasn't going to do the whole thing himself. The Lord would work through him, and Joshua would lead the people into victory after victory – but they had to fight.

That's the very thing that the Israelites didn't want to do. In Numbers 13-14 we read that the people heard that there were giants in Canaan, and they were afraid to go in and do battle with nations like the Amalekites. They would have much preferred that the Lord do some sweeping miracle and clear out the land ahead of them *without* their help!

But God uses people to do his work; it's one of his "ways," the ways that he accused the Israelites of not knowing (see Hebrews 3:7-19). He has certain things that *he's* going to do, because we can't do them – the miracles, for example. But he then assigns certain things for his people to do. He doesn't give them anything that they can't do. Or, if the task is impossible, what he wants from them is to march off into battle anyway and trust God to go in front of them and destroy what they can't handle – like the city of Jericho.

Jesus promised to give us Heaven, the eternal Promised Land. But he doesn't intend to give it to people who want to lean back and watch him do all the work. There is work to do, and we are supposed to get busy with the duties he has given us. Has he given us a talent of responsibility? Then he expects to see the profit we made from it when he returns to take us to Heaven. Has he given us opportunities to visit the sick and those in prison, to clothe the naked and feed the hungry? Then he doesn't want to hear excuses on the Last Day about why we didn't do our job, or didn't even know what our duty was. (Matthew 25)

We are called "fellow workers" with Christ (1 Corinthians 3:9), and work we must. There is a lot to do! We have our own souls to work on; we have our neighbor to help; we have God to glorify and help to build his Kingdom on earth; we have the enemy to fight. If someone can't see the work that's to be done, they are either immature spiritual babies or they are blind. In either case they are "worthless servants" to the Lord (Matthew 25:30) and he won't be satisfied until they grow up, change their ways, and start taking part in the work of the Kingdom.

Jesus *could* do it all without us – he could just speak the word and we would all be in Heaven right now, enjoying eternity – but he prefers to work *through us*. Then when he shares the glory of the throne of Heaven with us, we will also feel the shared responsibility of that throne and glory in the God who includes us in his Kingdom as sons and heirs.

- **<u>Joshua brought the people back to God.</u>** At the end of his life Joshua gathered the people together and renewed the covenant that the Lord had made between himself and Israel. As you read the story, however, you get the idea that Joshua had the same sober opinion of the Israelites as Moses did. He knew that they could easily be faithless and treacherous, and turn their backs on their promises to the Lord. He even told them so!

> Joshua said to the people, "You are not able to serve the LORD. He is a holy God; he is a jealous God. He will not forgive your rebellion and your sins. If you forsake the LORD and serve foreign gods, he will turn and bring disaster on you and make an end of you, after he has been good to you." (Joshua 24:19-20)

But Joshua wasn't just being plain with them about their hearts. He also wanted to see them saved. Knowing how easy it was for them to forget God and serve idols, he wanted to "put the fear of God in their hearts" and show them how prone they were to getting themselves into spiritual danger. Now that they were safe in the Promised Land, it would be a shame to put it all in jeopardy – which wasn't an idle threat, by the way, since God meant what he said when he told them he would take it away from them if they rebelled against him. So Joshua brought the people back to the covenant and the Law, and made them face the seriousness of the agreement they had made with their God. They stood to lose the whole thing if they didn't remain faithful to their commitment.

This reminds us of the many warnings that Jesus made to his followers. They too must take their commitment seriously; they couldn't presume on God's good graces and sin away their privileges. Sinners will be punished, no matter what they call themselves. Did someone work hard in Christ's name and yet wasn't careful to live a life of holiness? The Lord will tell them on Judgment Day – "I never knew you. Away from me, you evildoers!" (Matthew 7:23) He warned us that "he who stands firm *to the end* will be saved." (Matthew 10:22) He doesn't want anybody quitting on him in the middle of the job, for whatever reason – "No one who puts his hand to the plow and looks back is fit for service in the kingdom of God." (Luke 9:62)

Christ is faithful, and fully capable of keeping us safe from all trials, troubles, enemies, sins, curses and dangers. Paul assured us of that. (Romans 8:38-39) But he is not responsible for our sin, nor will he overlook willful rebellion. It won't help someone in the least on Judgment Day to claim that Jesus saved them if all they had on their record is willful rebellion against their God. We are to be *saved* from our sin – so that, by the time we get to Heaven, we're supposed to be able to show some progress in that area.

That's why there are serious warnings all through the New Testament writings about being careful about our salvation. (See 2 Corinthians 13:5; Philippians

2:12; 2 Peter 1:10) Though the Lord has brought us into a good land, and we are now heirs of God's righteousness and treasures of Heaven, we do not have the freedom to take all that goodness for granted and disobey him. (Romans 6:1-4) He will most certainly make us wish we hadn't had such foolish thoughts!

The Temple

**Then God's Temple in Heaven was opened, and within his Temple was seen the ark of his covenant.
(Revelation 11:19)**

In Bible times the Temple was the most important spot in Israel. It was the center of all their religious activities: they offered their sacrifices there, the priests ministered before the Lord there, and the Israelites came from all over the country to gather there three times a year for the annual feasts.

But probably the most important reason that the Temple was so crucial for the life of the Jews was that *their God lived in the Temple*. If they ever wanted to find him and talk to him, he could be found here. That's why the destruction of the Temple (twice – once at the Exile in 586 BC, again in 70 AD by the Romans) was so devastating to the Jews. Without the Temple they had no contact with God.

But the earthly Temple was only a symbol, a shadow of the real one in Heaven. The Temple in Jerusalem was designed to teach us about how to approach God, and how to worship him. But the Jews weren't supposed to confuse the shadow for the reality. It pointed forward in time to when all of God's people would learn to come to God in Heaven, to his Temple there, and worship him in Spirit. The Temple in Heaven is the real gathering place for God's people.

What is a temple?

To us, a temple is a strange idea. Though our church buildings could give us a faint picture of what the Temple might have been like, they can't come close to showing us the drama of God's Temple – the sound of worshipers praying and singing, animals braying and bleating, the sights and smells of blood and incense and burning flesh on the altar, priests and other people constantly coming and going between the courtyards day and night. It was a very graphic and unforgettable scene.

The Temple started out as a large tent that Moses and the Israelites built during their wanderings in the wilderness. But they weren't allowed to build it any way they pleased. God gave them specific instructions on what materials to use and how to put them together. For example, here is a description of some of the smallest details in its construction:

> For the entrance to the courtyard, provide a curtain twenty cubits long, of blue, purple and scarlet yarn and finely twisted linen — the work of an embroiderer — with four posts and four bases. All the posts around the courtyard are to have silver bands and hooks, and bronze bases. The courtyard shall be a hundred cubits long and fifty cubits wide, with curtains of finely twisted linen five cubits high, and with bronze bases. All the other articles used in the service of the tabernacle, whatever their function, including all the tent pegs for it and those for the courtyard, are to be of bronze. (Exodus 27:16-19)

God didn't leave anything to chance or the imagination of man. He wanted every detail just so. The reason is amazing: the earthly Temple was supposed to faithfully reflect every detail of the original Temple of Heaven.

> They serve at a sanctuary that is a copy and shadow of what is in Heaven. This is why Moses was warned when he was about to build the tabernacle: "See to it

that you make everything according to the pattern shown you on the mountain." (Hebrews 8:5)

God wanted to build an exact replica of the Heavenly Temple in Jerusalem, down to the smallest detail, so that his people would learn how to worship him *in truth*. Here they would practice, so to speak, with a model made of stones and silver and gold for the day when they would enter the one "not made by hands" in Heaven.

In fact, it was so important that Moses and the builders get it right that the Lord gave his Spirit to those who would be overseeing the construction of the Temple:

> Then the LORD said to Moses, "See, I have chosen Bezalel son of Uri, the son of Hur, of the tribe of Judah, and I have filled him with the Spirit of God, with skill, ability and knowledge in all kinds of crafts — to make artistic designs for work in gold, silver and bronze, to cut and set stones, to work in wood, and to engage in all kinds of craftsmanship. Moreover, I have appointed Oholiab son of Ahisamach, of the tribe of Dan, to help him. Also I have given skill to all the craftsmen to make everything I have commanded you." (Exodus 31:1-6)

One of the functions of the Spirit is to reveal the things of Heaven to us so that we can know and understand what God and his world are really like. So, if the Israelites are to have an exact replica of the Temple of Heaven, they would have to have the Spirit reveal it to them first. In this way the Lord would ensure that the two would be identical – not that the one in Heaven is made out of materials found on earth, but the earthly Temple faithfully represents the spiritual reality of the one in Heaven.

The Israelites came here to the Temple if they wanted to worship God. We are so used to going to whatever church is handy for our worship that we often fail to realize how important this single building was to the Jews. They weren't allowed to offer sacrifices anywhere else in the kingdom; in fact, they often got into severe trouble for even trying. By God's Law, the Temple in Jerusalem was the only place they could bring their sacrifices. If that meant they had to travel from Dan (over 100 miles to the north of Jerusalem) or from Beersheba (over 40 miles to the south) then that's what they had to do.

This is why some of the Psalms are called "songs of ascent." For example, look at Psalm 122 – the subtitle says "A song of ascents. Of David." This is because Jerusalem was built on the hills of Israel, and most Israelites had to climb up the hills to get to it. And the Temple itself was built on one of the peaks in the city. So they had to *ascend* the hill to go to the Temple:

> I rejoiced with those who said to me,
>   "Let us go to the house of the LORD."
> Our feet are standing
>   in your gates, O Jerusalem.
> Jerusalem is built like a city
>   that is closely compacted together.
> That is where the tribes go up,
>   the tribes of the LORD,
> to praise the name of the LORD
>   according to the statute given to Israel.
> There the thrones for judgment stand,
>   the thrones of the house of David. (Psalm 122:1-5)

God had a throne in the Temple; it was in the very center of the building, and one had to go through several courtyards and behind a curtain to get to it. In that center room – called the Holy of Holies – was the ark, a wooden box covered with gold and covered with statues of cherubim. The ark was the Lord's seat from which he ruled over Jerusalem. All worship was directed toward this throne.

But when Solomon built the first Temple in Jerusalem, he realized that such a building, no matter how grand, couldn't hold the Almighty God. He knew that there was another purpose of the Temple:

> But will God really dwell on earth with men? The heavens, even the highest heavens, cannot contain you. How much less this temple I have built! Yet give attention to your servant's prayer and his plea for mercy, O LORD my God. Hear the cry and the prayer that your servant is praying in your presence. May your eyes be open toward this temple day and night, this place of which you said you would put your Name there. May you hear the prayer your servant prays toward this place. Hear the supplications of your servant and of your people Israel when they pray toward this place. Hear from Heaven, your dwelling place; and when you hear, forgive. (2 Chronicles 6:18-21)

He put his finger on the essence of God's Temple. We all know that any building on earth, no matter how magnificent, can't contain the Creator. To him the earth itself is just a speck of dust! But the idea of the Temple is that his Name will be there. When we need him, we simply turn toward his Temple and call his Name – then he will hear us and answer us from the Temple. It's a simple idea yet a very powerful one, especially for us who now must turn toward the Temple in Heaven for our answers.

A Temple in Heaven

Though the lessons that the Israelites learned from their Temple in Jerusalem were extremely important, they weren't supposed to get the wrong idea from them. God never intended for anybody to fix their hopes on an earthly Temple. He always did live *in Heaven*, not on earth, and he wants us to turn there if we want to find him:

> The God who made the world and everything in it is the Lord of Heaven and earth and does not live in temples built by hands. And he is not served by human hands, as if he needed anything, because he himself gives all men life and breath and everything else. From one man he made every nation of men, that they should inhabit the whole earth; and he determined the times set for them and the exact places where they should live. God did this so that men would seek him and perhaps reach out for him and find him, though he is not far from each one of us. (Acts 17:24-27)

The Temple is a controlled environment, so to speak. The Lord requires that we approach him *in a certain way.* The Law, spelled out for us in Genesis, Exodus, Leviticus, Numbers, and Deuteronomy, makes it very plain to us how to worship him. He requires certain words, certain sacrifices, a certain attitude, certain clothes. Anybody who deviated from the strict ceremony that he laid out in the Law was to be put to death – as even Aaron's sons discovered!

> Aaron's sons Nadab and Abihu took their censers, put fire in them and added incense; and they offered unauthorized fire before the LORD, contrary to his command. So fire came out from the presence of the LORD and consumed them, and they died before the LORD. Moses then said to Aaron, "This is what the LORD spoke of when he said: 'Among those who approach me I will show myself holy; in the sight of all the people I will be honored.'" Aaron remained silent. (Leviticus 10:1-3)

You don't trifle with God Almighty! If he says that *this* is how you will worship him, then we have an obligation to stick to the ceremonies that are written in his Law.

The various elements of the Temple (the lampstand, altar, incense, ark, courtyards, veil, table of bread, basins, and so on) were designed to address the spiritual needs of God's people. Here they would find their sin washed away, they would get food for their souls, they could get answers to their prayers – and, most important, they would be able to see how glorious and awesome God really is. Walking through the courtyards, and watching the sacrifices, and hearing the prayers of the priests, and seeing the blood shed all around, was intended to solemnly impress the worshiper and get him in the right frame of mind to communicate with God.

Of course God set this system up on purpose to get that response from us. Anybody who comes to the Lord must do it in the right frame of mind, with the right attitude of humility and awe and reverence and hope. It's a place where we can be assured, by what we see and do there before him, that God will receive us and answer our prayers.

What is going on there now?

The Temple of Heaven is a busy place. For some reason we tend to think that Heaven is a static region out beyond the universe where everything is peaceful, calm and unmoving. On the contrary! If the Temple in Jerusalem was continually busy with sacrifices and prayers, we will find its original in Heaven even busier. The needs of the entire world are being addressed there day and night. Nothing stops in Heaven, because people are constantly approaching the throne of grace for help from the Lord.

The Temple of Heaven is not a museum! The Old Testament shows us what is there now, in Heaven, that we can take advantage of now. If the rules about using them are a bit different for us than they were for the Israelites, that doesn't mean that we are to ignore them. *This is still the way that God expects his people to approach and worship him.* The difference is that now Jesus is taking care of the demands of the Law for us; we need only follow him into the Temple, into the Holy of Holies, and present our requests to the Father based on the Temple preparation work that he does for us.

Jesus offered himself as **the sacrifice for sin** in the Temple. There were a lot of different sacrifices in the Old Testament Temple, but every one of them reflected something about the overall sacrifice of Christ. What he did for his people was so huge, so complex, that it took many Old Testament laws to teach us about his work. Now, when we go to the Temple ourselves, we pass the blood on the altar, we smell the offering of incense rising up to God, we see the grain offering and the flesh of the firstborn – all aspects of the sacrifice of Christ that God demands of us.

There in the Temple in Heaven **we present our requests to God**. We must do just as Solomon knew we must – we must turn toward God on his throne, in the Holy of Holies, and call on his Name. He will then hear us and give us what we ask for. Isn't this exactly what Jesus said to do?

> In that day you will no longer ask me anything. I tell you the truth, my Father will give you whatever you ask in my name. Until now you have not asked for anything in my name. Ask and you will receive, and your joy will be complete. (John 16:23-24)

Since the Lord dwells in his Temple, we must go there to find him and get what we need. The Temple is just as important and necessary for our Christian faith as it was for the Israelites. We are not permitted to seek the Lord in any other place, nor worship him anywhere we please. Our duty is to come to him in the Temple and offer our prayers and sacrifices; then he will hear us, according to his promise.

God's throne in the Temple is also a **judgment seat**. The King rules from Heaven, and he examines the hearts of all his subjects – to their very thoughts and attitudes.

> For the word of God is living and active. Sharper than any double-edged sword, it penetrates even to dividing soul and spirit, joints and marrow; it judges the thoughts and attitudes of the heart. Nothing in all creation is hidden from God's sight. Everything is uncovered and laid bare before the eyes of him to whom we must give account. (Hebrews 4:12-13)

He continually judges his creation to make sure that it is headed in the direction he wants for it. All of history, and all the parts of his universe, serves his eternal purposes, and it will all turn out in the end as he intended from the beginning. The Judge is going to see to that.

The **Word of God** also comes out from the Temple. The priests had two responsibilities: first, to take the sacrifices that the people brought and present them to God; second, to bring back God's Word and blessing to the worshipers who were waiting out in the courtyard. God speaks through his servants the priests and the prophets, so that his people can know his mind exactly.

Finally, it's there in God's Temple that we must **worship** him. Worship is filling your mind and heart with the reality of God, and responding to him appropriately. Worship is giving him the credit he deserves. Through worship we learn to humble ourselves in his presence, throw ourselves upon him completely, learn his will, give thanks for what he has done, and get Heavenly resources to live our lives in his service.

Can we come to this Temple?

It was easy to go to the Temple in Jerusalem. It was a physical building in a particular spot on earth. And it was required by Law, upon penalty of death, for every Israelite to show up at the Temple during the annual feasts to worship God.

But since our Temple is in Heaven now, can we go there ourselves? Isn't Heaven – a spiritual place not in this world – a bit out of our range? Can God really expect us to show up there when we are still bound to earth? Is the Temple therefore only reserved for after this life?

No, the Temple worship is for now. We are expected to show up in the Temple regularly, just as the Israelites were. God wants to see us there at his throne, because there are many matters to be taken care of now that can't wait until the end of time. Jesus taught that it is not only possible, but mandatory, that we come to the Temple *in Heaven*:

> Believe me, woman, a time is coming when you will worship the Father neither on this mountain nor in Jerusalem. You Samaritans worship what you do not know; we worship what we do know, for salvation is from the Jews. Yet a time is coming and has now come when the true worshipers will worship the Father in spirit and truth, for they are the kind of worshipers the Father seeks. God is spirit, and his worshipers must worship in spirit and in truth. (John 4:21-24)

When the Temple in Jerusalem was destroyed in 70 AD, the Temple of Heaven officially took its place. Now everyone who calls on the Name of the Lord must turn to Heaven and pray; otherwise they will get no answers. The blood that saves us is on the Heavenly altar, not on earthly ones.

How are we, being physical creatures, expected to get to that Temple in Heaven? The key is the Holy Spirit. The Spirit lifts us up spiritually into the presence of God. While our bodies remain on earth, spiritually we are brought into God's Temple so that we can see and use the things that are there. Hebrews shows us this graphically:

> But you have come to Mount Zion, to the Heavenly Jerusalem, the city of the living God. You have come to thousands upon thousands of angels in joyful assembly, to the church of the firstborn, whose names are written in Heaven. You have come to God, the judge of all men, to the spirits of righteous men made perfect, to Jesus the mediator of a new covenant, and to the sprinkled blood that speaks a better word than the blood of Abel. (Hebrews 12:22-24)

Notice that it doesn't say that we *will* come (as if we have to wait until we die and go to Heaven before we can see it) but that we *have* come. Our worship *now* brings us into Heaven. And it's not our imagination! If we were only imagining what is in the Temple, we wouldn't be able to take advantage of the articles that we see there. In order to get forgiveness of our sin, we have to have that blood sprinkled on our hearts. In order to be cleansed from guilt, we have to wash in the basin of water provided for us there. In order to get answers from God for our needs, we have to walk through the torn veil and meet God sitting there on the ark of the covenant, face to face. It has to be real, not imagination. So the Spirit actually does take us there to be with God in his Temple. True worship couldn't happen otherwise.

There are several places in the New Testament where we are counseled to worship in the Spirit:

> I tell you the truth, no one can enter the kingdom of God unless he is born of water and the Spirit. Flesh gives birth to flesh, but the Spirit gives birth to spirit. (John 3:5-6)

Yet a time is coming and has now come when the true worshipers will worship the Father in Spirit and truth, for they are the kind of worshipers the Father seeks. God is Spirit, and his worshipers must worship in Spirit and in truth. (John 4:23-24)

For it is we who are the circumcision, we who worship by the Spirit of God, who glory in Christ Jesus, and who put no confidence in the flesh. (Philippians 3:3)

True worship can't happen apart from the work of the Spirit. He *reveals* the things of Heaven, all the parts of the Temple there and how to use them; and he *empowers* us to reach out and take advantage of what's there.

So, in answer to the question as to whether we can worship in this Temple of Heaven – we had better! If we don't, we won't get anything from the God of Israel. He insists that any who worship him turn toward his Temple and call on his Name. In other words, even in our modern generation, we need a Temple too – it's not just an ancient ceremony. Salvation and life are there.

Fellowship with God

One of the encouraging lessons of the Old Testament is that *God wants to live with his people.* He is coming to earth to set his throne among the Israelites. No other nation on earth had been so honored up to this time.

Living with God means living with the **Creator**. He made everything, and he keeps everything alive and moving. He provides for the daily needs of all his creatures (see Psalm 115). So if the Israelites are in need of anything – and who could set a limit on what God can do? – all they have to do is come to the God who lives in their midst and ask him.

Living with God means living with pure **righteousness**. Sin is the terrible and destructive force on earth that makes life so miserable and, in the end, brings death. Wouldn't everyone on earth love to be able to solve this problem of sin and death! Now the Israelites have that opportunity. They can – and are even commanded to – come to the Redeemer who knows how to fix the problem. He can not only cleanse us of sin, but he can undo the damage that sin has done to us in the past and "repay you for the years the locusts have eaten." (Joel 2:25)

Living with God also means that you are living with the **King**. The King rules all; the entire universe is under his hand, and he makes the decisions for mankind that are worked out in history. But the Israelites found themselves called up to the highest place in the universe – they were God's representatives on earth. Even the angels aren't allowed into the secret counsels of God that the Lord will share with his people! They are his children, and therefore heirs of the treasures of Heaven. They are given the wisdom of God, which means they will understand the importance of God's glory, the problems that must be solved in God's universe, and how to build up his Kingdom on earth.

David knew the bliss of living with God. In his own writings he longed to be close to God in God's house; here is Psalm 84:

> How lovely is your dwelling place, O LORD Almighty! My soul yearns, even faints, for the courts of the LORD; my heart and my flesh cry out for the living God. Even the sparrow has found a home, and the swallow a nest for herself, where she may have her young – a place near your altar, O LORD Almighty, my King and my God. Blessed are those who dwell in your house; they are ever praising you. Blessed are those whose strength is in you, who have set their

hearts on pilgrimage. As they pass through the Valley of Baca, they make it a place of springs; the autumn rains also cover it with pools. They go from strength to strength, till each appears before God in Zion. Hear my prayer, O LORD God Almighty; listen to me, O God of Jacob. Look upon our shield, O God; look with favor on your anointed one. Better is one day in your courts than a thousand elsewhere; I would rather be a doorkeeper in the house of my God than dwell in the tents of the wicked. For the LORD God is a sun and shield; the LORD bestows favor and honor; no good thing does he withhold from those whose walk is blameless. O LORD Almighty, blessed is the man who trusts in you.

You can tell by this that he found tremendous comfort and strength in being close to God. To him, the Temple wasn't a religious chore to carry out but a spiritual bonus.

The theme of God living among his people, and they living in his house, is an important hope and blessing of the Church. The pomegranates and other garden themes of the Temple hearken back to the Garden of Eden (**Genesis**) where man and God lived together. The **Song of Songs** describes the close relationship between lover and beloved. Jesus said that when two or three gather in his Name, he will be among them – **Matthew 18:20**. John loves the fellowship he has with Jesus and the Father, and wants all Christians to share in that fellowship – **1 John 1:3**. In **Revelation 21:1-3** we get a glimpse of the holy city where God will live with his people. Paul describes the Church as the Body of Christ in **1Corinthians 12**, because we are so close we actually become one with him and he with us. The reason that God and we are so close is because he has sent his Spirit to live inside us – **John 14:17; 1 Corinthians 3:16; Ephesians 2:22; 2 Timothy 1:14; 1 John 3:24**. And that is what Paul calls the mystery of the Gospel – **Colossians 1:27**.

The descriptions of the Tabernacle and the sacrificial system here in the Old Testament are symbols, or shadows, of the real Temple in Heaven. There is a Temple in Heaven – God lives there, and there is where his subjects approach him if they want to relate to him. Heaven is the real destination for all of God's people; it's been the plan that the Church would live with God forever in Heaven since the world was made. But (as we learn in the Old Testament laws) we must relate to this God in a certain way. We can't just run up to him and do and say as we like to him! We have to learn the house rules, and show the kind of respect that he deserves in all of our dealings with him. That's what the Temple in Heaven represents – it's the meeting place where we will relate to God. The Old Testament is simply a preview of what it will be like there in Heaven.

The elements of a true sacrifice

The sacrifices that the Mosaic Law required were critical for the welfare of the people of God. They form the foundation of what it takes to be forgiven of our sins – a reality that we Christians take very seriously. In fact, they are part of God's eternal plan for dealing with sinners. One surprising example of how the sacrificial laws extend to all of God's people is in the story of Abel, who actually lived *before* the Mosaic Law spelled out the details of a true sacrifice that God would be pleased with.

Abel's sacrifice consisted of the very elements that would achieve the purpose of a right sacrifice – forgiveness of sin. Through faith he saw what God is most interested in – our sin – and what God requires of us to get us out of legal trouble with the Law. These are the elements in Abel's sacrifice:

> **Blood** – To be an acceptable sacrifice to God, something must die. The Law demands the death of the sinner; it's serious about righteousness, and it

leaves no room for sinners in God's righteous kingdom.

> In fact, the Law requires that nearly everything be cleansed with blood, and without the shedding of blood there is no forgiveness. (Hebrews 9:22)

This element teaches us a lot about what's going on between God and ourselves: it shows us that we are sinners, it shows us how seriously God takes our sin, it shows us how horrible and destructive our sin is in God's Kingdom to warrant our death sentence, and it shows us the love of God that he would kill another in order to save us from this same horrible end.

A substitute – By God's mercy, he allows us to bring a substitute to his throne to die in our place. We don't have to die for our sins, though. We certainly deserve to die for them. But instead of giving us what we deserve (and again we have to notice here that there is nothing we could ever do to appease God, we deserve only death from him) he makes someone else (or in the case of an animal, some*thing* else) bear the burden of our punishment.

> When Aaron has finished making atonement for the Most Holy Place, the Tent of Meeting and the altar, he shall bring forward the live goat. He is to lay both hands on the head of the live goat and confess over it all the wickedness and rebellion of the Israelites — all their sins — and put them on the goat's head. He shall send the goat away into the desert in the care

of a man appointed for the task. The goat will carry on itself all their sins to a solitary place; and the man shall release it in the desert. (Leviticus 16:20-22)

We can't forget, either, that the substitute – be it goat or sheep or the Son of God – experiences the full punishment that would have been ours had God been less gracious to us.

The firstborn – In an amazing insight due to his faith, Abel saw the eternal principle in God's Kingdom that the *firstborn* must die for the sins of others. The Law made this same provision later on during Moses' ministry:

> Consecrate to me every firstborn male. The first offspring of every womb among the Israelites belongs to me, whether man or animal. (Exodus 13:2)

But that again is only because the Law looked even further on in history to the time when God's Firstborn – Jesus Christ – would become the sole sacrifice for the sins of the world. The cross of Christ was the focal point of all the sacrifices offered up to God throughout history. All of those sacrifices only have meaning when they reflect the offering of Jesus' own body on Golgotha. Since the Old Testament saints didn't have the benefit of looking *back* to Christ's sacrifice as we do, they must look *ahead* to it; in other words, they had to use some way of showing that their sacrifice is acceptable to God *in Christ*. The way they did this was to use the firstborn of the flock.

Atonement – Even if Abel had carried out the first three steps of a true sacrifice, he wouldn't have gotten the response he was looking for from God if this last step didn't happen. Atonement means to *cover over* one's sins so that God doesn't look at us as if we are sinners. The blood of the substitute, the firstborn, is acceptable material for what must be done next – to cover over the sins in our hearts.

> For the life of a creature is in the blood, and I have given it to you to make atonement for yourselves on the altar; it is the blood that makes atonement for one's life. (Leviticus 17:11)

Because the whole point of sacrifice is to escape the condemnation of the Law, the solution is to make us righteous in God's sight. And since that isn't going to happen on our efforts – we *can't* be righteous as God requires it, no matter how hard we try to follow his Law – the solution is to cover our sinful hearts with the blood of the sacrificial victim, so that God sees clean, holy people instead of former rebels and wicked sinners.

The Name is there

This brings us to one of the most tragic aspects of Jewish history. The special name of God in the Old Testament – YHWH (Hebrew יהוה), or as we put it, the LORD — was unique to the God of the Israelites. This was the Name that he gave them to use when they worshipped him; this name distinguished him from other gods. He even poured tremendously important meaning into that Name (see Exodus 34:6-7). But over the centuries, because of an overly zealous respect for the holiness of God's special Name, the Jews made up rules about it. First, nobody was allowed to speak that Name; it was too holy for a sinner to even pronounce and make dirty with his sinful lips. Second, whenever the rabbi was reading in the Bible and he came to this holy Name, he was not to pronounce it even then — he was to say "Adonai" instead and go on around it. Third, the scribes, when they wrote their books of interpretation of the Biblical text, weren't even supposed to write the holy Name. The only way they could represent it was to write the first and last letters only, like this: Y"H. Furthermore, the problem was compounded by the fact that Hebrew didn't have any vowels — for *any* word, let alone the holy Name. So all they had were the consonants: YHWH.

The result was that, over time, everyone forgot how to pronounce God's special Name! Nobody, not even the scholars, could remember what the vowels were supposed to be. In their fanatical zeal to preserve the holiness of his Name they ended up with a Name they couldn't even use!

What makes this even more tragic is that this was the Name that God told them to call on if they wanted to be saved! "Everyone who calls on the Name of the Lord will be saved." (Joel 2:32) If they refused to even pronounce it, how could they hope to be saved?

We Christians aren't superstitious about his Name like the Jews were. But we have our own problems about his Name: we don't even think about using it. We think there's no power or benefit in using it. So we also don't call on the Name of the Lord. That's what Jesus was referring to when he accused his disciples: "Until now you have not asked for anything in my Name." We have these vast resources at our disposal, these handles to the door of Heaven, and we don't use them. We leave behind the very things that he told us will get his attention and his interest.

The Temple

"The LORD will hear when I call to him." (Psalm 4:3) There's the promise. But there's the responsibility too: if you address him by Name then you can expect to get somewhere with the Lord. Otherwise, forget it.

Just like anybody who turns around to face us when we call their name, the Lord will do the same with us when we call him by his special names. He knows that he is the *only* one we could be referring to! Nobody else can rightfully claim the full meaning of that Name.

There are many Scriptures that quote God's promise to us that he will answer when we call on him. But probably the most powerful example of how he responds to his Name is found in the story of the Temple that Solomon built. Read the story once and you may miss the significance of what God is saying about this temple; read it a few more times and this idea of his Name starts becoming more obvious:

> I have chosen and consecrated this Temple so that my Name may be there forever. My eyes and my heart will always be there. (2 Chronicles 7:16)

Solomon understood from the very beginning that this was to be the place where God's Name would be:

> But will God really dwell on earth with men? The Heavens even the highest Heavens, cannot contain you. How much less this Temple I have built! . . . May your eyes be open toward this Temple day and night, this place of which you said you would put your Name there. May you hear the prayer your servant prays toward this place. (2 Chronicles 6:18,20)

In other words, his Name has a place near us — where we can take hold of it, call on him with it in prayer, and be assured that he will "hear from Heaven, your dwelling place." (2 Chronicles 6:21) God had the Temple built just for this purpose!

Jesus once claimed that his Body is a Temple. (John 2:19-21) Who will be able to enter into that Temple for eternal life? Only the ones who call upon his Name; the same principle is in operation there:

> I have revealed your Name[1] to those whom you gave me out of the world ... Holy Father, protect them by the power of your Name — the Name you gave me — so that they may be one as we are one. (John 17:6,11)

The One through whom we may be saved has come close to us, "closer than a brother," close enough to touch him and hear him, so that we can call on him and be saved. "The Word is near you; it is in your mouth and in your heart." (Romans 10:8) This proves God's intention to answer when we call his Name.

---

[1] It's unfortunate that the NIV Bible didn't translate what the Greek original says here. The word "name" is in the original text, but the translators didn't see the importance attached to God's Name in this context. But when we consider the tremendous importance attached to God's Name elsewhere in Scripture, and how Jesus refers several times to God's Name in this very prayer, then we must insist that the English translation include the word.

The Kingdom of David and Solomon

**I have found David son of Jesse a man after my own heart; he will do everything I want him to do.
(Acts 13:22)**

David inherited a mess from King Saul. Under Saul's leadership, Israel fell to her lowest point since some of the disastrous days of the Judges. For centuries, the Israelites had been used to doing whatever they thought was right, without any one person leading the people back to the Law to find out what God wanted them to do.

In those days Israel had no king; everyone did as he saw fit. (Judges 21:25)

When Saul was king, Israel had hopes that for once the people would be drawn into a single nation under one head, and they would be able to defeat their enemies and prosper for a change. And at first it seemed that this would happen: Saul won victories over the Philistines. But it wasn't long before Saul showed the true nature of his heart. He began to disobey the Lord's commands and do things his own way. For example, when Samuel passed on the Lord's command to put every living creature in the Amalekite camp to death, Saul evidently thought that this was an unnecessary waste – so he saved the livestock, and even spared the life of the Amalekite king. When Samuel found out that Saul hadn't carried out his orders, the Saul made the excuse that

> The soldiers brought them from the Amalekites; they spared the best of the sheep and cattle to sacrifice to the LORD your God, but we totally destroyed the rest. (1 Samuel 15:15)

But God isn't interested in our opinions; when he gives us a command to carry out, he expects strict obedience:

> Does the LORD delight in burnt offerings and sacrifices as much as in obeying the voice of the LORD? To obey is better than sacrifice, and to heed is better than the fat of rams. For rebellion is like the sin of divination, and arrogance like the evil of idolatry. (1 Samuel 15:22-23)

Obviously Saul wasn't going to work out as the king over God's people. The Lord needs someone for the job who will be careful about the Law of Moses, someone who is filled with the Spirit and knows the mind of God, someone who is primarily interested in God's glory and not his own.

So the Lord sent Samuel out to find a replacement, which he found in the shepherd boy David, the eighth son of Jesse. At the time not even his own family – not even the prophet Samuel himself! – thought that this young boy would measure up to the exacting requirements of this job. But the Lord saw something in David:

> The LORD does not look at the things man looks at. Man looks at the outward appearance, but the LORD looks at the heart. (1 Samuel 16:7)

David, the Lord could see, was "a man after his own heart" (1 Samuel 13:14) who would work to build God's Kingdom, not his own, over the Lord's people.

David the King

When David took over as King (you can read about the ceremony in 2 Samuel 5:1-5) he immediately set about working on five critical areas:

- **First, he established a capital city.** The Jebusites, Canaanites who had remained unconquered from Joshua's day, held the fortified hilltop called Jerusalem and dared David to conquer them. They underestimated him. He took it from them and made it his official residence. The story is in 2 Samuel 5:6-10.

    The king needed a capital for a central location for his realm. Up until this time, even in Saul's day, the center of government was wherever the judge or king happened to live – and that changed frequently. The Israelites from Dan to Beersheba had no one place to bring their problems or concerns to.

    David, however, made his kingdom much easier to manage and deal with by setting up his throne in Jerusalem. His subjects brought him tribute there, came there for his judgments, and gathered there for the religious festivals. He himself sat on the throne in Jerusalem and sent out his officers from there over the entire nation to carry out his commands. In fact, the city of Jerusalem became identified with the King – it was known as the "holy" city because of it being the seat of the King and the place where God also lived in the Temple.

    Setting up Jerusalem as the capital was probably the single most important factor in bringing stability to the nation. Up until this time Israel was just a collection of confused, warring tribes who couldn't pull themselves together to work on anything. But now in one stroke David had turned Israel into a nation in her own right with a king to be reckoned with – with the resources of a nation behind him, both for war and for peace.

- **Second, David finally crushed the enemies of Israel.** For too long the Israelites had been persecuted, harassed and defeated by her pagan neighbors. The book of Judges is a graphic example of her history: because she hadn't exterminated all the Canaanites living in the land, Israel repeatedly suffered at their hands. The Lord would raise up Judges to save them from their oppressors, but in a short time the Israelites would go back to worshipping the false gods of their neighbors, and God would punish them with wars and persecution.

    At first it seemed that King Saul was going to break the cycle of war and oppression – he did win a few victories over their enemies in the beginning – but when he fell into sin and rebellion himself the Lord again allowed the Israelites to suffer defeat, especially at the hands of the Philistines.

    When David ascended the throne, the time had come to put this issue to rest – permanently. As you can see in 2 Samuel 5, he promptly went to battle against the Philistines and the Moabites and defeated them. What he did to the Moabites shows us how determined he was to settle the issue for good: he put to death two thirds of the men of the nation, in a harsh way! That act alone no doubt impressed the Israelites that they finally had a leader who could deal summarily with the enemy – their foreign policy problems were over.

- **Third, he led the people back to God.** Another problem in Israel is that the pure worship that Moses laid down to them in the Law was almost a thing of the past. Several stories in Judges show us that the people of God had seemingly forgotten how to worship the Lord – false priests, altars to foreign gods, immorality, no justice. The ark traveled around the country side – it was at Bethel, or at Shiloh, or carried into battle with the army. The religion of the Lord God of Israel seemed to be of little importance to the people. Even the priests – for example, Eli and his notorious sons – treated the service of the Lord as an opportunity for personal gain.

It was time to bring the Israelites back to their God. In 2 Samuel 6 we read of David bringing the ark from the house of Abinadab into the city of Jerusalem. After the little problem about Uzzah touching it without authority (and getting put to death for his trouble!) David and the people entered Jerusalem and set up the ark in the tent on Mt. Zion. It was a magnificent ceremony – dancing, singing, worship, food and drink – and it was purposely designed to impress the people with how central the Lord and his worship were to the nation. Whatever the other nations might do, Israel must come together around her God in praise and worship, obeying his Law, offering the stated sacrifices for sin and atonement. David made it a state institution of his new Kingdom.

The important thing to grasp is that David had to step in and restore the worship of the Lord; because, being the head of the state, he had the authority as well as the responsibility to provide an example of what the Israelites must do to please God. The nation will do as the King does; so if David goes back to the Lord, so will his people. And he went on to lead the people again and again to the Lord in worship, as we can see from his many psalms.

- **Fourth, he established a government.** David was only one man. Though he set up Jerusalem as his capital and sat on the throne of Israel, he couldn't go himself and execute the laws of his Kingdom from Dan to Beersheba.

He needed a system of government, administrators and officials to carry out his orders.

He made his sons government officials, because he could exert the necessary influence over them to carry out his will. He also had many trusted friends and army comrades whom he made government officials – see the list of some of them in 2 Samuel 8:15-18. These were men who came out to David when he was an outlaw in the wilderness, hiding from Saul's unjust wrath. Men like these needed to be rewarded for their loyalty.

Of course he wouldn't have picked fools for important government posts. He knew the skills of each man and put them in the places where they would do the most good for the nation. David's goal, remember, is to build up Israel in the fear and knowledge of the Lord. So he is going to make sure that whoever he has in authority over the various aspects of Israel's life will help build that kind of Kingdom.

And the rule of his government was the Law of God. The man who wrote the following lines –

> The Law of the LORD is perfect, reviving the soul. The statutes of the LORD are trustworthy, making wise the simple.
>
> The precepts of the LORD are right, giving joy to the heart. The commands of the LORD are radiant, giving light to the eyes.
>
> The fear of the LORD is pure, enduring forever. The ordinances of the LORD are sure and altogether righteous.
>
> They are more precious than gold, than much pure gold; they are sweeter than honey, than honey from the comb.

By them is your servant warned; in keeping them there is great reward. (Psalm 19:7-11)

... knew how important it would be to live by God's Law as a nation, not just as an individual. To David it would never be a problem of deciding what was the right or just thing to do, or what justice would be – it's all written in God's Word.

- **Fifth, he prepared the plans and materials for the Temple.** Many people think that Solomon, since he built the Temple, must have drawn up the plans for the Temple. They are mistaken. It was David who drew up those plans. Not only that, he also gathered the materials for the Temple. When he was about to die, he handed over the entire project to his son Solomon – so that all that Solomon had to do was follow the instructions that his father had left him!

David at one point had wanted to build a Temple for the Lord; it bothered him that he had a fine palace to live in while the ark of the Lord was still sitting in the old, original tent that Moses had made hundreds of years ago. But the Lord had someone else in mind as the builder of the Temple. David, the Lord told him, was a man of blood:

> You have shed much blood and have fought many wars. You are not to build a house for my Name, because you have shed much blood on the earth in my sight. (1 Chronicles 22:8)

Not that what David had done was wrong (it was God who gave him victory over his enemies), but that the hands which built this special House must be those of a man of peace.

> But you will have a son who will be a man of peace and rest, and I will give him rest from all his enemies on every side. His name will be Solomon, and I will grant Israel peace and quiet during his reign. He is the one who will build a house for my Name. He will be my son, and I will be his father. And I will establish the throne of his kingdom over Israel forever. (2 Chronicles 22:9-10)

In fact, the name Solomon comes from שָׁלֹם – Shalom – which means "peace." The Temple is where God will dwell among his people in peace – peace between God and man, and between man and man.

But David was going to play an important role in the Temple. The Lord showed him what the Temple must look like, what it must be made of, and even the personnel required to work in the Temple and what their duties were.

> "All this," David said, "I have in writing from the hand of the LORD upon me, and he gave me understanding in all the details of the plan." (1 Chronicles 28:19)

This was appropriate for two reasons: *first*, because David had a special relationship with the Lord and knew the heart of God. God shared his thoughts and plans with David so that he could rule over the Israelites in truth, according to God's Law. So he had an insight into God's ways and works that would result in the kind of Temple that would be acceptable to God.

Second, he is the model king for Israel, and what he's doing through his realm would be the pattern for all the kings to follow – especially for the Messiah, the Son of David who would sit on David's eternal throne. For this reason the Lord appointed David as the architect of the Temple – for the sake of the work on God's spiritual Temple that Jesus would later build, as the Son of David.

David had his share of problems in life, some of them caused by his own sin and foolishness (for example, his adultery with Bathsheba and cover-up murder of her husband). And the Lord certainly punished David for his sins; not even the King of Israel is above the Law. But even when he sinned, he proved that he had the kind of heart that God wants to see in his servants. For example, in Psalm 51 we see a sinner in the agony of guilt and repentance for his sin. The Lord showed himself a merciful God in how he handled the great sins of David.

The point, however, about David is that he successfully accomplished the five tasks that made Israel a great nation under God. Here was a people who lived by God's Law, who treated each other with justice and righteousness, who trusted in God to take care of them, and who regularly came to God's throne for worship and submitting themselves to his will. What more could God want out of a people than this? They were in a perfect position for him to bless them and lead them – and David got them there when generations of leaders and kings before him failed to do so.

David ruled over Israel for forty years. Being mortal, the time came to turn over the kingdom to his son Solomon and die. But as it says in Ecclesiastes, we can work hard all of our lives and then turn over our estates to someone who just may mess everything up!

> I hated all the things I had toiled for under the sun, because I must leave them to the one who comes after me. And who knows whether he will be a wise man or a fool? Yet he will have control over all the work into which I have poured my effort and skill under the sun. This too is meaningless. So my heart began to despair over all my toilsome labor under the sun. For a man may do his work with wisdom, knowledge and skill, and then he must leave all he owns to someone who has not worked for it. This too is meaningless and a great misfortune. (Ecclesiastes 2:18-21)

Fortunately Solomon was the wisest man of his age – so he managed to preserve the Kingdom that his father left him. In fact, he made Israel the richest nation in that area, certainly richer than she had ever been or ever will be, and there was peace along all of her borders during his reign. It was Israel's height of glory. But even Solomon had his faults that laid the seeds for future problems:

> As Solomon grew old, his wives turned his heart after other gods, and his heart was not fully devoted to the LORD his God, as the heart of David his father had been. (1 Kings 11:4)

There are two important things to notice in this passage. *First*, David is used as the pattern, the model king of Israel, with whom all his descendants were compared. In other words, David's works were fundamental to the life of Israel and the glory of God. Any king who succeeded him must do as his father David had done in order to get God's approval.

And that's the *second* thing to notice here – all the descendants of David who sat on the throne of Israel *were* compared to their ancestor David. Here even Solomon strayed from the royal program that God expected his kings to follow:

whereas David led the people back to God, Solomon began leading them away from God to worship false gods. You see? The Scriptures judge a king by whether they followed the five-point plan of David, the model king.

Other kings were judged in the same way:

> He committed all the sins his father had done before him; his heart was not fully devoted to the LORD his God, as the heart of David his forefather had been. (1 Kings 15:3)

> He did what was right in the eyes of the LORD, but not as his father David had done. (2 Kings 14:3)

> He did what was right in the eyes of the LORD, just as his father David had done. (2 Kings 18:3)

The last example was Hezekiah. He was one of the few kings of Judah who got a 100% approval rating from the Lord. And as you can see here, the Lord approved of him because he "did as his father David had done."

The Son of David

The Scriptures call Jesus the Son of David. For example, these passages use that name when referring to him:

> A record of the genealogy of Jesus Christ the son of David, the son of Abraham. (Matthew 1:1)

> As Jesus went on from there, two blind men followed him, calling out, "Have mercy on us, Son of David!" (Matthew 9:27)

All the people were astonished and said, "Could this be the Son of David?" (Matthew 12:23)

The crowds that went ahead of him and those that followed shouted, "Hosanna to the Son of David!" (Matthew 21:9)

While the Pharisees were gathered together, Jesus asked them, "What do you think about the Christ? Whose son is he?" "The son of David," they replied. (Matthew 22:41-42)

It was a popular concept – one which these and other passages emphasize – that the Messiah would be not only a descendent of David but would sit on David's throne, ruling over David's kingdom. There's a good reason for that. Many people could claim to be descendants of David; even Joseph, Jesus' so-called "step-father," was a "son of David." But the Messiah would actually rule over the kingdom that was given to David – *and do the same things that his father David had done.* This is the key to understanding the ministry of Christ as he set up his kingdom.

Let's go back through the five-point plan of David and see if Jesus followed it in his own ministry.

- **First, he established a capital city.** Jesus also needs a central location for his government, and a place to set up his throne from which he will rule his kingdom. His disciples, in fact most of the Jews of his time, thought that the Messiah would march into downtown Jerusalem and set it up there. But they misunderstood what kind of Kingdom that Jesus came to set up – it would be a *spiritual* kingdom, not an earthly one.

Jesus said, "My kingdom is not of this world. If it were, my servants would fight to prevent my arrest by the Jews. But now my kingdom is from another place." (John 18:36)

So he wasn't interested in downtown Jerusalem. He left this world and ascended the throne in Heaven, at God's right hand. From there he rules over his kingdom, which extends beyond the borders of the land of Canaan to include people and nations all around the globe, all through time. His position there in Heaven gives him the vantage point of power, authority, glory and majesty. His coronation story is recorded in Psalm 2.

Now whoever wants to see the King must ascend the steps of the heavenly Mt. Zion and approach the throne that sits above all earthly thrones. It's a spiritual world, there where Jesus reigns; the location was chosen specifically so that Jesus could accomplish all that he had in mind. In this world he set aside his glory, and limited his works to individuals and places close at hand. But in the Jerusalem in Heaven he is free to extend his Kingdom to whatever places he chooses, which includes the human heart.

- **Second, he crushed the enemy.** The time had come to deal conclusively with the enemy. So Jesus confronted the primary enemy – Satan – head-on, as soon as he was anointed from on high:

    Then Jesus was led by the Spirit into the desert to be tempted by the devil. (Matthew 4:1)

And just as David confronted Goliath, the champion of the Philistines, with a surprising weapon which in God's power proved the undoing of the enemy, Jesus confronted Satan with the Word of God and sent him running. From that point on, it will only be a matter of time until all the dominions that lay under the hand of Satan and his followers will be either destroyed or taken away from them by this new King:

> The reason the Son of God appeared was to destroy the devil's work. (1 John 3:8)

This has to be done, because God's people need some relief from the enemy of their souls. It's impossible to be about the business of repentance, salvation, and holy living as long as we have a persistent foe constantly tripping us up and destroying everything we do. We need some protection from him, and some peace from the battle, so that we can follow Jesus. So Christ deals with the enemy for us while we tend to the matters of our soul.

- **Third, he led the people back to God.** Sin is rebellion against God's Law. As it says in the Bible, "sin is lawlessness." (1 John 3:4) And everyone is guilty of sin. This means that the entire human race has turned its back on its Creator and is following its own feelings and opinions, instead of carrying out the orders that God gave us as his servants.

So another essential work of the Son of David is to turn us around and bring us back to the God we left. We must find God; we can't afford to live without him any longer. And Jesus takes several measures to do this: *first*, he reconciles God to us – he took our punishment upon himself so that God can't hold anything against us any more. Because of what Christ did for us on the cross, the Lord now looks upon us with favor – if we come under the shadow of that cross and let the blood from that death cleanse our souls.

Second, he fills us with his Spirit who turns our path toward Heaven. We are now God's children, destined to live and rule with him in Heaven forever. But before we assume such a high role in the universe, we have to be made fit for the job. So the Spirit is going to lead us into holiness, give us skill at kingdom-building, put our minds on the matters of Heaven, reveal the new world to us to motivate us, and so on. The Spirit is Christ's Spirit (see Romans 8:9; Philippians 1:19; 1 Peter 1:11). So when Jesus said to "follow me" (Matthew 16:24), he meant to follow the leading of his Spirit within you (Galatians 5:18,25). He himself, through his Spirit, will lead you into Heaven where God is –

> I am the way and the truth and the life.
> No one comes to the Father except through me. (John 14:6)

- **<u>Fourth, he established a government.</u>** Being the Son of God, I'm sure that Jesus could very easily administer his entire Kingdom without our help. In this way he differs from his father David – who literally couldn't do the entire thing himself.

But one of the ways that God likes to do things is to use people to do kingdom work, even though he wouldn't have to. Paul says that we who work with the King are "fellow workers" (1 Corinthians 3:9) through whom he rules his kingdom.

Jesus made promises to his disciples that they would be part of his government administration. It wasn't going to be exactly what they expected – they thought they would rule as the Gentiles do, in power and impressive majesty. Instead, Jesus' administrators would be servants living for the benefit of others:

> You know that the rulers of the Gentiles lord it over them, and their high officials exercise authority over them. Not so with you. Instead, whoever wants to become great among you must be your servant, and whoever wants to be first must be your slave – just as the Son of Man did not come to be served, but to serve, and to give his life as a ransom for many. (Matthew 20:25-28)

Nevertheless he put together a government complete with officials carrying out his orders and administering his grace to the people. The entire system of spiritual gifts in the Church is the government of Heaven at work:

> But to each one of us grace has been given as Christ apportioned it. This is why it says: "When he ascended on high, he led captives in his train and gave gifts to men" … It was he who gave some to be

apostles, some to be prophets, some to be evangelists, and some to be pastors and teachers, to prepare God's people for works of service, so that the body of Christ may be built up until we all reach unity in the faith and in the knowledge of the Son of God and become mature, attaining to the whole measure of the fullness of Christ. (Ephesians 4:7-13)

We can see in this passage the kingdom of Christ at work: each of his officials, the people with spiritual gifts in the Church, carry out his will for the benefit, well-being and growth of the Kingdom.

And we can be sure, since Christ rules over his kingdom by sending out his Spirit, that everything will be done according to God's holy standard of righteousness. It will be a Kingdom of Law and order, righteousness and justice – and a great deal of mercy. As Paul tells us in Romans –

> ... in order that the righteous requirements of the Law might be fully met in us, who do not live according to the sinful nature but according to the Spirit. (Romans 8:4)

- **Fifth, he laid the foundation for the Temple.** If Jesus' kingdom is ruled from Heaven, if the capital city of Jerusalem is in Heaven, we can therefore expect that the Temple itself would also be in Heaven.

When Moses first made the Tabernacle, he was instructed to make it like the Temple that was in Heaven:

> Make this tabernacle and all its furnishings exactly like the pattern I will show you. (Exodus 25:9)

> They serve at a sanctuary that is a copy and shadow of what is in Heaven. This is why Moses was warned when he was about to build the tabernacle: "See to it that you make everything according to the pattern shown you on the mountain." (Hebrews 8:5)

And that's why we are told, whenever we pray, that we are in reality coming into the Temple in Heaven – into God's very presence as he sits on his throne in the Temple in Heaven. We saw this already in Hebrews 12:22-24.

So while Jesus was on earth, he had in mind the building of the Temple of Heaven. The plans for it were constantly in his mind, and he gathered materials for that Temple. We know this by some hints that he gave us along the way. For example, he called his disciples to follow him so that he could make them "fishers of men." (Matthew 4:19) The role that the disciples would play in the Kingdom of God was going to be crucial: it was their testimony of what they saw in Christ that we now have in our Bibles. Their writings became, quite literally, the foundation of the Church of Christ.

Consequently, you are no longer foreigners and aliens, but fellow citizens with God's people and members of God's household, *built on the foundation of the apostles and prophets*, with Christ Jesus himself as the chief cornerstone. In him the whole building is joined together and rises to become a holy Temple in the Lord. And in him you too are being built together to become a dwelling in which God lives by his Spirit. (Ephesians 2:19-22)

This passage, in fact, graphically illustrates what Jesus had in mind when he chose the apostles to carry the message to the world. Everyone who believes that message becomes part of the House of God, the Temple where God lives among his people. Jesus had them in mind too, during his ministry:

I have other sheep that are not of this sheep pen. I must bring them also. They too will listen to my voice, and there shall be one flock and one shepherd. (John 10:16)

His intention is to draw all of his people together, from all parts of the globe and across all of time, into one Temple where God will live with them. The people of God are the building materials, the stones, out of which the Temple will be built:

As you come to him, the living Stone – rejected by men but chosen by God and precious to him – you also, like living stones, are being built into a spiritual house to be a holy priesthood, offering spiritual sacrifices acceptable to God through Jesus Christ. (1 Peter 2:5)

So you see that Jesus was planning and collecting for the Temple during his entire ministry, just as his father David had done.

Keep in mind that since the Old Testament Scriptures judged the descendants of David by comparing what they did with the works of their father David, we must also look at the works of Christ in the same light. He can justifiably lay claim to the title "Son of David" *only if* he did the same things as David had done.

The Prophets

They have Moses and the Prophets.
Let them listen to them.
(Luke 16:29)

One of the things that causes the bitterest fights in the Church today is the subject of prophecy. That's really unfortunate, because the prophecies were given to us so that we might have hope (2 Peter 1:19), not discouraging fights! If people can only fight about it and separate from each other about it, that only shows that they aren't getting the *point* even though they might know the *facts*.

Rather than starting with the many issues involved, let's start at the beginning. If we lay a good groundwork for our study of prophecy, by looking carefully at Scriptural principles, we can be more certain that what we end up believing about prophecy will be true. If the foundation is good, the rest of the building has a better chance of being good.

What is a Prophet?

Most people think of a prophet as someone who predicts the future. Certainly the Prophets in the Bible predicted future events. In fact, the Lord made it plain that any prophet who predicted some future event that did not come to pass is a false prophet and was not sent by the Lord! (Deuteronomy 18:22)

But simply predicting the future doesn't make a prophet what he is. Stock market analysts can predict the future too, and so do weather specialists. Prediction was a side issue; there was something much more important about the job of the Bible's prophet that made his role critical in God's Kingdom.

Perhaps we can get closer to an understanding of what a prophet is if we first look at man's problem. Paul tells us that every one of us are (or have been) subjects of the powers of darkness; we have willingly "followed the ways of this world and of the ruler of the kingdom of the air, the spirit who is now at work in those who are disobedient." (Ephesians 2:2) Rather than knowing God, as we were created to do, we know nothing about God; in fact, our abysmal ignorance of God is the very reason we live in such wickedness and fall into suffering and death so easily.

Physically speaking, man has lived under the rule of many types of governments and kingdoms. Some have been good, some bad. But none of them have been able to address the problem of man's sinful heart. No matter how much law we impose on the outside, the heart of man rebels at righteousness and prefers to do things his own way, *not* God's way. "This only have I found: God made mankind upright, but men have gone in search of many schemes." (Ecclesiastes 7:29) Of course this has brought people to their many miseries: "The wages of sin is death." (Romans 6:23) Death comes in many forms: physical, spiritual, psychological, economical, intellectual, and so on — but all of them share the same devastation and pointlessness.

All this and more happens because man refuses to live under the rule of God.

> The kings of the earth take their stand and the rulers gather together against the Lord and against his Anointed One. 'Let us break their chains,' they say, 'and throw off their fetters.' (Psalm 2:2-3)

And if God doesn't rule this earth, then what will? The passions of men, of course, and ignorance, and rebellion, and whatever dark powers over us that can take advantage of our confusion. When God isn't running things, the result is "sexual immorality, impurity and debauchery; idolatry and witchcraft; hatred, discord, jealousy, fits of rage, selfish ambition, dissensions, factions and envy; drunkenness, orgies, and the like." (Galatians 5:19-21) The result is this: what once used to be a peaceful, serene kingdom with happy subjects (we're describing the original Creation, of course) is now a ruined battleground with struggling opponents fighting over what isn't worth having anymore.

The solution: A new kingdom

The Lord God Almighty isn't going to look down on a rebellious earth for long. He made this place, it belongs to him, and he is determined to rule over it. He gave man a chance to obey him and we wouldn't; now he is going to get what he wants through another method.

In Isaiah 9 we read a prophecy that tells us what God is going to do:

> For to us a child is born, to us a son is given, *and the government will be on his shoulders.* And he will be called Wonderful Counselor, Mighty God, Everlasting Father, Prince of Peace. Of the increase of his government and peace there will be no end. He will reign on David's throne and over his kingdom, establishing and upholding it with justice and righteousness from that time on and forever. The zeal of the Lord Almighty will accomplish this. (Isaiah 9:6-7)

This prophecy is about Christ, of course. Don't miss the point, however! It isn't simply predicting that Jesus would come; it is telling us *what will happen* when Jesus comes: the Kingdom of God. He is coming to assume control; he will sit in the throne and rule over us. The times of men doing their own thing will come to an end, and from that point on he will *rule*.

When Jesus rules, things happen. For once there is justice, because he will make sure everyone gets their just reward and punishment. He can do that because he is the Judge, able to see into our hearts and discern what is really there; he isn't fooled by outward appearances as we are. He saves people from what is destroying them — their sin. He fills their hearts with the Spirit which will lead them in the way of life for a change, a way of holiness that pleases God. Jesus also defeats our enemies, as any good king should, so that we are free from the tyranny of the world, the flesh, and the devil and can settle down peaceably to live our lives for him. When Jesus reigns, peace settles over the people, they enjoy life, the wicked are thrown out, and God gets the glory that is his due.

That's the prophecy — but did it happen? Check out the stories in the Gospels to see if these things came true. You will find that this prophecy was completely fulfilled there: not among the Jews, nor the Gentiles, but among the believers, the followers of Christ. Not everyone had eyes to see this new kingdom: "The knowledge of the secrets of the kingdom of Heaven has been given to you, but not to them." (Matthew 13:11) "I tell you the truth, no one can see the kingdom of God unless he is born again." (John 3:3) Simeon saw it (Luke 2:30), the disciples saw it (Luke 10:23), but most of Jerusalem didn't see this new kingdom. (Luke 19:42) Nevertheless, the Kingdom of God finally arrived in the reign of Christ in the Church.

Notice *where* we got the description of the kind of kingdom that Jesus would set up: from the prophet Isaiah. In fact, if you read through the prophets of the Old Testament, you will begin to find a common theme running through them all: they not only *predict*, they not only *confront* us with God's Word, they also **reveal the coming kingdom of God.** Each prophet is showing us what God intends to do in the future. The Lord is going to tear down the kingdoms of this world, destroy the works of the devil, and shake out what he didn't create. Then when he has thoroughly destroyed all competition, he is going to set up his kingdom in their place. All the prophets deal with this subject in one form or another.

And we could go on and on, quoting the prophets as they described this kingdom that God was going to set up. They predicted what it would be like when God runs things, both positively and negatively. Some long-standing problems are going to get solved for good! The wicked will be dealt with forever; the righteous will be able to breathe free again. The world is going to run like God wants it to run for a change.

The Spirit of Prophecy

How did the Prophets know what the kingdom would be like? God showed them. Through the Spirit, the Lord showed the prophets what would happen when the Lord came to rule over earth. The prophets didn't make any of this up, nor did they guess what the Lord would do. This is, in other words, the *Word of God* — that's why we are counseled to pay attention to what the prophets are saying:

> And we have the word of the prophets made more certain, and you will do well to pay attention to it. (2 Peter 1:19)

> Above all, you must understand that no prophecy of Scripture came about by the prophet's own interpretation. For prophecy never had its origin in the will of man, but men spoke from God as they were carried along by the Holy Spirit. (2 Peter 1:20-21)

Every prophet of God was moved by the Spirit of God to say what he said. This means a couple of things: *first*, what he had to say was a message told him by the Spirit; he wouldn't have known the subject or the right words if the Spirit hadn't told him. *Second*, the situation he was facing — the need of the people he was speaking to — was something that only the Spirit of God understood. The Lord could see into the people's hearts and therefore knew the message to tell them. The prophet himself could never have figured out either of these things on his own.

You will find the Spirit of God involved in the message of every single prophet in the Bible:

> As he spoke, the Spirit came into me and raised me to my feet, and I heard him speaking to me. (Ezekiel 2:2)

> On the Lord's Day I was in the Spirit, and I heard behind me a loud voice like a trumpet. (Revelation 1:10)

> Belteshazzar, chief of the magicians, I know that the spirit of the holy gods is in you, and no mystery is too difficult for you. (Daniel 4:9)

> Then the Lord came down in the cloud and spoke with him, and he took of the Spirit that was on him and put the Spirit on the seventy elders. When the Spirit rested on them, they prophesied, but they did not do so again. (Numbers 11:25)

Why is the Spirit of God involved in every one of the prophets? If you understand the special work that the Spirit does, the mystery clears up: God's Spirit *reveals* the hidden things of God so that we can see what we didn't see or understand before. Paul describes this in Corinthians:

> We have not received the spirit of the world but the Spirit who is from God, that we may understand what God has freely given us. (1 Corinthians 2:12)

The Spirit opens our spiritual eyes so that we can see God's world. For example, Jesus told Pilate that he was a king, though his kingdom wasn't of *this* world — but Pilate couldn't see that or understand it at all. (John 18:36-38) But when the Spirit revealed the same truth to the Roman centurion, he saw Jesus as the Master, who is able to command disease with authority. (Matthew 8:5-13)

The Lord sent his Spirit upon the prophets for some very good reasons:

- ***Dead-on accuracy*** — When any man thinks he has something to say to the hearts of his hearers, he can only hope that he gets it right; he doesn't really know what is in their hearts like God does. But when a prophet spoke to people, he *knew* what was in their hearts because the Spirit showed him. He was able to say exactly what they needed to hear from God; there wasn't any guessing about it. This means that the people *had* to listen to the words of the prophet because it was *straight from God*.

  So do we. The Lord spoke through the prophets to us as well, and we have to take their message seriously. "And we have the word of the prophets made more certain, and you will do well to pay attention to it, as to a light shining in a dark place, until the day dawns and the morning star rises in your hearts." (2 Peter 1:19) This may sound surprising to "New Testament" Christians who never look in the Old Testament for much of anything. But it's true that the Lord has much to say to you through the message of the prophets.

- ***A spiritual kingdom*** — The prophets spoke of the kingdom of God; that much we can see. But when you think about it, a kingdom where God rules has to be totally different from any kingdom that this world has seen. "God is Spirit, and his worshipers must worship in spirit and in truth." (John 4:24) If we want to see our King, we have to have spiritual eyes to see him; if we want to hear what he has to say, the Spirit has to give us the ability to hear with our spirits. God rules from Heaven, which is a spiritual place (not like this physical earth) and he is building, right now, a kingdom on earth (called the Church) where the Lord rules and takes care of his people. All of this is of a spiritual nature, not physical like the kingdoms of this world.

So when the prophets spoke about the kind of kingdom that God had in mind to set up among men, you will find them talking about very spiritual things happening: like righteousness, seeing God's glory, changing the heart, and so on. They never said that God would rule on a physical throne, covered with gems and gold like an earthly king, wielding a physical sword over his enemies! The Jews didn't appreciate the spiritual nature of God's kingdom when Jesus showed up and claimed to be a king. They thought that, if he were really a king, he should start acting like one! They didn't understand his "spiritual" approach to the kingdom.

- *<u>Correct interpretation of events</u>* — The prophet "saw" circumstances differently than other people did. Most people think that circumstances in our lives, even strange circumstances, are just Mother Nature at work. The prophets, however, saw the hand of God, because the Spirit opened their eyes to be able to see God's work. So when they told the people what was really going on and why, the people should have accepted their interpretation.

For example, when the Israelites were suffering under the military might of foreign empires like Egypt and Babylon and Assyria, they tended to see it as we would:

they hated their enemies and longed for the day when they would get out from under their control. But the prophets who spoke the Word of God to them during those centuries had an entirely different interpretation of the events: this was the hand of God, using their enemies to punish them for their sins. "O LORD, you have appointed them to execute judgment; O Rock, you have ordained them to punish." (Habakkuk 1:12) Instead of hating their enemies, they should have been humbling themselves before God because of their sins that he was punishing them for. We need the message of the prophets to tell us the correct way to think about what happens to us in life.

- **_Reveals the mind of God_** — A prophet, since he spoke what the Spirit showed him, is really telling us the very thoughts of God. And that is exactly what the Spirit does: "The Spirit searches all things, even the deep things of God. For who among men knows the thoughts of a man except the man's spirit within him? In the same way no one knows the thoughts of God except the Spirit of God." (1 Corinthians 1:10-11)

This is important because we need God to tell us what he is thinking; we can't continue to make up stories about what God is like. We have so many opinions about God and what his will is! Has nobody ever asked God himself to see what he thinks? Do you think he will sit around and let us make up ridiculous theories about him, without ever getting up and proclaiming the truth about himself and silencing all arguments forever? This is exactly what he has done through the prophets; these words, these messages are on God's heart, and these are the things that are important to him, the things he intends to do on earth. We do not need to guess or wonder about what he thinks anymore. And we ought not to ignore it either! Someday these things that the prophets spoke about will come true.

The role of the Prophet

We've seen the *definition* of a prophet, and the *qualifications* of the prophet. Now we're ready to look at his message and learn about the job he's been given to do. The prophets of the Lord had four parts to their message:

The Message of the Prophet

- **War**
- **Law**
- **Judge**
- **Messiah**

- <u>**Prophecy: A message of war**</u> – The Prophet was like an emissary sent out ahead of the king with his army, to parley with the enemy and demand a surrender. The Lord has had enough of the wicked destroying his Kingdom and rebelling against his Laws. He's coming to put down the rebellion and set up a righteous Kingdom. But he sends out a Prophet ahead of the army, to warn the rebellious that war is coming, and they had better surrender *now* if they want to find mercy. Otherwise they can expect none.

- <u>**Prophecy: Upholding the Law**</u> – The standard of righteousness that God has always wanted to see in his Kingdom was the Law given through Moses at Mt. Sinai. This is the description of righteousness; this is God's condemnation of sin; this is the remedy for sinners seeking mercy from the King. The Prophets took the people back to the Law of Moses and pressed the Lord's demand that they once again observe this Law.

- **Prophecy: The Judge speaks** – If anybody wants to know what Judgment Day will be like, let them read the Prophets! Here we find God scrutinizing our hearts with terrifying accuracy. He knows what we are – there is no hiding anything from him. When God examines our hearts using his Law for a standard, there is no more doubt that we have sinned against him to the extent that we need the unfathomable love of God to cover over those sins.

- **Prophecy: A spiritual kingdom** – The Israelites were proof that nobody can keep the Law. Not only were they incorrigible sinners, but as Hebrews tells us, "it is impossible for the blood of bulls and goats to take away sins." (Hebrews 10:4) What is needed – what God had planned all along from the beginning of the world – is a spiritual Kingdom where we will be truly cleansed and *stay* that way forever. We need a **Messiah** to come and do these impossible tasks for us.

The prophets were on an extraordinary mission. They saw God in his glory, received his Word from his own mouth, and were sent out by God to confront people with the Kingdom of

God. The words of the Prophet were the very words of God himself. To turn one's back on a Prophet is to throw away your last chance at salvation – which the Israelites found out to their shame and hurt!

The Prophets also had an insight into the Messianic Kingdom that was the solution to sin and death in this world. Though they saw the misery that mankind lives in, they also saw the answer in Jesus and his spiritual Kingdom. What the Law could never do on its own, the Messiah would do on a spiritual level – and do it so well that it would forever cure the problems of sin and death. It was time to switch from a faith in earthly things to the sacrifice of the Son of God for forgiveness, and eternal riches in Heaven. No wonder, then, that Jesus pointed people to the Prophets for the message of salvation!

> "I have five brothers. Let him warn them, so that they will not also come to this place of torment." Abraham replied, "They have *Moses and the Prophets*; let them listen to them." "No, father Abraham," he said, "but if someone from the dead goes to them, they will repent." He said to him, "If they do not listen to *Moses and the Prophets*, they will not be convinced even if someone rises from the dead." (Luke 16:28-31)

The two greatest Prophets

You may not have known this, but there were two prophets in Israel who were greater than any other prophets. Not just in how much they said, but *what* they said; not greater in *quantity* but in *quality*.

The first one was Moses. We read this about him in Deuteronomy:

The Prophets

Since then, no prophet has risen in Israel like Moses, whom the Lord knew face to face, who did all those miraculous signs and wonders the Lord sent him to do in Egypt — to Pharaoh and to all his officials and to his whole land. For no one has ever shown the mighty power or performed the awesome deeds that Moses did in the sight of all Israel. (Deuteronomy 34:10-12)

This is a high rating! When Moses' sister and brother tried to cut in on the act and get some glory for themselves, the Lord rebuked them and told them that Moses was special among the prophets. "With him I speak face to face, clearly and not in riddles; he sees the form of the LORD." (Numbers 12:8) There was a reason for this, which we will look at in a minute.

The other great prophet of Israel was Jesus Christ. Moses told us (of course!) that he would be coming: "The LORD your God will raise up for you a prophet like me from among your own brothers. You must listen to him." (Deuteronomy 18:15) Peter confirmed that this was Jesus in Acts 3:22.

Now what did these two men do that made them prophets? Just this: *they revealed the kingdom of God.* Only they did it in a big way! Let's begin with Moses. When the Israelites left Egypt they headed straight for Mt. Sinai. At this point they were still only a mob, blindly following Moses wherever he led them. When they got to Mt. Sinai they met their God — and there they found out that *he* was their real leader, not Moses.

The next forty years was a crash course on the kingdom of God. They learned his laws, they learned how to please him, they learned his plans for the future, they were fed and watered by him, they watched the miracles he did for their benefit. The Lord was making a people, a nation, out of these Israelites.

How did they learn all this? Remember that they were too afraid to get close enough to God to hear his voice! (Deuteronomy

5:23-27) Moses was the one chosen to take all the words of God to the people; as God built the nation Israel, he did it all through Moses. And the foundation that was laid during these forty years through Moses' ministry lasted for the next 1500 + years until the next major prophet could take over — Jesus.

When Jesus came, he too announced the kingdom: "The time has come, the kingdom of God is near. Repent and believe the good news!" (Mark 1:15) Only this time the kingdom was to be completely spiritual; nothing on earth could adequately represent the things in the kingdom of Heaven. He, like Moses, set up a nation of God's people where the Lord would rule over them and they would enjoy his blessings. In this kingdom, however, people were really saved from their sins! They ate spiritual manna from Heaven; they drank from the spiritual rock in the desert; they felt the Law penetrate their hearts in severe conviction of every thought and act; they received the Spirit who enabled them to obey God; they were protected from spiritual enemies; and so on. It's easy to see, in the work of Christ, a new world in the making; he was forming a new nation out of Jew and Gentile and creating the circumstances necessary for their happy life with God the King.

Moses and Christ were actually working on the same project, the same house, the same kingdom. After all, this is the kingdom of God — and he doesn't have two kingdoms but one. In Hebrews we find this:

> He was faithful to the one who appointed him, just as Moses was faithful in all God's house. Jesus has been found worthy of greater honor than Moses, just as the builder of a house has greater honor than the house itself. For every house is built by someone, but God is the builder of everything. Moses was faithful as a servant in all God's house, testifying to what would be

said in the future. But Christ is faithful as a son over God's house. (Hebrews 3:2-6)

This explains in a nutshell why these two prophets were so great — and what they were doing as "prophets." They were responsible for setting up the house, so to speak; through their ministry they revealed to the people the kind of world they were living in. Through their words, the people saw God in his holiness, in his love, in his anger, in his government, in his redemption, in his promises.

Keep in mind that Moses didn't actually do the work himself; God built his Kingdom through Moses. That's the role of the prophet: to reveal God in his glory coming to set up his Kingdom on earth. Jesus, however, is that King that the rest of the prophets predicted would come.

The Importance of the Old Testament

To give people the benefit of the doubt, I would say that most Christians dismiss the Old Testament mainly because they don't know what it teaches. Nobody taught them the important concepts of the book, so naturally they aren't interested in a book that confuses them.

But such a state of affairs is crippling the Church. There is no way that Christians can understand the New Testament when they are so clueless about the Old Testament. The writers of the New Testament relied heavily on the Old; they were continually quoting from it, using its lessons, sending people back to its pages to learn its lessons again. They even got frustrated (including Jesus, when he got so angry with the Pharisees and teachers of the Law who should have known better) because their students obviously hadn't done their homework first in the Old Testament; there were more lessons to learn, but that was impossible due to their ignorance of the basics of the faith.

Paul states that the Christian Church is built on both the teachings of the Apostles and the Old Testament prophets:

> Consequently, you are no longer foreigners and aliens, but fellow citizens with God's people and members of God's household, built on the foundation of the apostles and prophets, with Christ Jesus himself as the chief cornerstone. In him the whole building is joined together and rises to become a holy temple in

the Lord. And in him you too are being built together to become a dwelling in which God lives by his Spirit. (Ephesians 2:19-22)

The Bible tells one story – and the Old Testament is the first part of that story. It lays the foundation for us to understand the more complex level of spiritual understanding in the New Testament. It is, so to speak, a course titled "Jesus 101" in the Bible's overall series on that subject. We *need* this book to truly know how to trust in Christ our Savior.

We didn't get into nearly everything of importance in the Old Testament in this study. But you now have many of the important highlights to get the picture. With this information you can now link both Testaments together to see that single plan that God had in mind from the very beginning. And hopefully you will continue in your study of the Old Testament on your own. Just remember that, as you study, you will successfully understand what the book is saying to you if you keep Christ's words in mind.

You diligently study the Scriptures [*remember that he was referring to the Old Testament here!*] because you think that by them you possess eternal life. These are the Scriptures that **testify about me**. (John 5:39)

A Short Summary of the Old Testament

The Old Testament is a history book if it isn't anything else! On the surface it's a history of the Jews, the descendants of Abraham. On a deeper level, however, it's a history of God's special works in preparing for the Messiah – the Savior who would open up the gates of salvation and eternal life to all who will call on him, not just the Jewish race. And if you have eyes to see it, as you read through the history of the Old Testament you can see the skillful steps that God takes to prepare for that great event recorded in the New Testament.

The history of the Old Testament can be broken down into eight sections.

From the Creation

The first history recorded is how the world was made. It shows us that God made the world out of nothing, and it teaches us the methods that God used to create the world and everything in it. We also learn the purpose of all created things – to serve the Creator and glorify him. Man in particular is assigned the responsibility of overseeing God's Kingdom. And we will see these same methods of creation used over and over in the rest of God's works recorded in the Bible.

But we also learn why the world we have now isn't the perfect system that God created it to be – it's because of man's rebellion against God's Law. Because of his sin, Adam plunged the entire human race into sin and death. The entire world is suffering as a result. The problem of sin is global, infecting every civilization. God was justifiably angry at what man did to his perfect creation and, by means of the Great Flood, revealed one option for taking care of the problem: wholesale destruction. He not only has the right but the power to stop man's insanity and rebellion.

Abraham and his family

God's second option for taking care of the problem of sin is grace. He chose Abraham and made a covenant with him and his descendants forever. The covenant was a solemn promise on God's part to bless Abraham and his family with four things. That covenant was a family treasure, passed on down through generations of heirs. It was not meant to be shared by anybody outside of the family.

Abraham lived in the land that God promised to him and his descendants – Canaan (the future Israel). His son and grandson, Isaac and Jacob, also lived in Canaan as wanderers and aliens as did Abraham.

Jacob, though undeserving and a deceiver by nature, was blessed by God in all that he did – he grew immensely rich and prosperous through God's miraculous hand. He had twelve sons, who would be the pillars of the future nation of Israel. By means of one son's rise to power in Egypt (Joseph), Jacob and his family moved and settled there to escape a wide-spread famine that struck the Middle East.

For the next four hundred years the descendants of Abraham grew to number in the millions. Unfortunately they became slaves under powerful Pharaohs and were made to work on state projects under inhuman conditions.

The Exodus and the Conquest

God heard the cries of misery of the children of Abraham suffering in Egypt, and under the leadership of Moses he broke Egypt's hold on his people and led them out of their slavery. After the miraculous crossing of the Red Sea (where the Egyptian army was destroyed), they were led to Mt. Sinai in the desert.

There they received the Law. This was the beginning of the nation of Israel. God pulled them together under one government, and the Law was the rule of God's government over them. They became his people, and he became their God. He also revealed his special name Yahweh to them and promised that they would come to learn what that name means through personal experience.

God then led them, through Moses' and his brother Aaron's leadership, through the desert to the land promised to Abraham. On the way they learned how God works on behalf of his people: through miracles. But in spite of his faithfulness in his care of them, and the miraculous power that he exercised for their benefit, they repeatedly angered him with their unbelief.

It was because they failed the test and rebelled against following the Lord into Canaan that he turned them around and sent them back into the desert to wander for the next forty years. All the adults died off (except for a faithful few). When the first generation was gone, the Lord led their children back to Canaan and, under the leadership of

Joshua (Moses died at the edge of Canaan), swept across the Jordan River. Jericho was the first pagan city to fall – and it was destroyed by a miracle. For the next few years the Israelites moved north and south through Palestine killing the Canaanites and taking over the land and homes for themselves. Each tribe was allotted a particular portion of the land, and finally they could settle down in peace.

The Judges

The problem was that the Israelites didn't kill off all of the Canaanites, and what God predicted would happen did happen. The surviving Canaanites led the Israelites into worship of idols and false gods. But in God's Kingdom, worship of false gods is going to bring a swift and painful punishment. God sent various nations against Israel in war and the Israelites suffered terrible defeats, sometimes being under foreign rule for decades in abject poverty.

But when they would come to their senses and turn to the Lord for help, he had mercy on them and send them a deliverer. These deliverers were called Judges, and usually they would raise armies to fight the foreigners. The Spirit of God obviously empowered the Judges to win the battles; the results could only be described as miraculous deliverances.

The weakness of this period of Israel's history was that the twelve tribes operated as twelve political units, instead of one nation. They refused to come together under God's rule; instead they wanted to rule themselves as they saw fit. The whole situation was inherently unstable.

It wouldn't be long until the next generation would fall back into the same sins of idolatry and immorality and plunge the tribes into defeat and oppression. The cycle started all over again, and somewhere down the road God would send another Judge to deliver his people when they had had enough of suffering.

David and Solomon

The Israelites came to realize that this lifestyle was not acceptable. They wanted a king to draw all twelve tribes into a nation that could defend itself against its enemies.

The Lord, however, knew that even that wouldn't be good enough. Their real problem was that they were rejecting *him*. At first, however, he gave them what they wanted – the first king of Israel, Saul. In the beginning he seemed to be just the answer they were looking for: they started winning battles against the enemy, and the tribes began pulling together under him and looking to him for leadership. But soon Saul himself began rebelling against God. He was a reflection of the spiritual sickness of the whole nation, and his rule was proof that a simple political answer of a king wasn't good enough for God's people.

David, however, a shepherd boy, was a "man after God's own heart." The Lord chose him to be king after the Israelites had lost Saul in battle. Now they would see what God wanted in a ruler: a man who would lead the people of God back to God; a man who himself bent his knee in submission to the Lord, who is the King of kings.

David immediately set about working on five necessary reforms: a capital city, defeat of the enemies of Israel, a government over all the tribes of Israel, leading the people back to God and true religion, and preparing for the building of the Temple. His agenda became the pattern that defined what God expected of all the succeeding kings of Israel; each of them were compared to their father David to see if "they had done as their father David had done."

David left a secure and strong kingdom to his son Solomon. Solomon extended the borders of the kingdom, made the nation rich and prosperous, and through his strong hand made Israel a land of peace. He also took the plans of the Temple that David had drawn up and built a house of worship for God's people. Israel reached the peak of her glory under David's and Solomon's rule.

Two Kingdoms – the Sons of David

But Solomon had enemies. The Northern tribes had never quite gotten over their misgivings of having a man from Judah, a tribe in the south, ruling over them. Under Jeroboam's leadership they rebelled against Solomon's son Rehoboam and split off to form their own nation. Thus began a split history of God's people: Israel in the north, and Judah in the south.

The trouble with Israel was that they refused to submit to David's sons (the rightful heirs of David's throne) and chose their own rulers instead. What was worse, since they would never come south to worship God in the Temple in Jerusalem, they set up golden idols in key locations in their own cities and started their own forms of worship. Baal was a favorite god of theirs. Of all their kings, Ahab (and his wife Jezebel) was the worst for the spiritual damage he did to God's people.

It was during this period that the Prophets came on the scene. Starting with Elijah, the Lord sent messengers to his people to warn them about their idolatry and immorality. Being merciful, he sent not just one but many prophets with the same message: repent now, or be destroyed when the Lord comes in his anger to tear down the idolatrous kingdom and set up a new righteous kingdom in its place. But instead of listening to the prophets, the Israelites ignored them and went on in their sin.

The end came in 722 BC. Hordes of warriors from Assyria swept through Israel, killing, burning, and carrying off captives. The custom in those days was to carry the population of a defeated nation back home and repopulate the area with foreigners – this to prevent any future rebellion. So Israel ceased to be a nation; the few Israelites left in the north ended up marrying the new foreigners and Jewish blood got mixed with Gentile blood. This was, in fact, the birth of the Samaritans – the hated breed of mixed marriages that the Jews of Jerusalem despised in the New Testament times.

Meanwhile, in the south, things weren't going much better. Judah managed to keep David's descendants on the throne in Jerusalem, but they too rebelled against God and the true worship of the Temple. Again, God sent them prophet after prophet with warnings to repent or perish. After years of rejection, God finally brought the Babylonians in 586 BC to destroy Jerusalem. The slaughter was horrific: the Temple itself was destroyed, thousands killed, thousands of others carried off into Exile to Babylon. As the prophet described it, God brought 70 years of needed rest from idolatry and immorality to the Holy Land.

The Exile

The Jews who were deported from Judah and Jerusalem actually stayed together in Babylon, unlike their brothers from the northern tribes who were scattered and lost. They learned to survive in Babylon under their new masters. In fact, they had a lot of time on their hands, and they used it profitably – they thought a lot about what went wrong back home. They saw that they angered God with their idolatry, and they went back to the Law and decided to take it more seriously.

Some of the most devout Israelites in history lived in exile in Babylon – Daniel, Shadrach, Meshak, Abednigo, Esther, and Mordechai. And God blessed them while they were in exile with leadership positions under their masters. He even protected them from disasters – for example, during Esther's lifetime the Lord kept the entire Jewish race from being wiped out by their enemies.

The Restoration from Exile

The Jews finally learned their lesson, and after 70 years in exile the Lord brought them back home to Jerusalem. Ezra, a priest who was a scholar "well versed in the Law of Moses," and Nehemiah, the governor of Jerusalem, led the people back and rebuilt the city and the Temple.

At first it was touch-and-go for the Jewish remnant. There were still enemies around who wanted to see the Jews completely destroyed. And the some of the Jews themselves put the whole project of rebuilding the land in jeopardy when they started marrying out of the faith – and bringing idolatry back into the picture. But when those problems were addressed firmly, they managed to settle down into peace and go back to the worship that Moses laid down in the Law.

The Jews became experts in the Law. They decided to take it seriously – to the letter this time. They began building up an "oral tradition" that extended the Law of

Moses to meet modern needs of society. But they went too far to the other extreme this time. By the time that Jesus came on the scene, the Jews (especially the Pharisees) had built up such a complex maze of man-made additions to the Law (supposedly to help them keep the Law better) that it was worthless for the needs of the soul. Their blind adherence to the letter of the Law was actually keeping them away from God. Jesus found a blind and obstinate people who could not hear the living Word of God from Heaven. Essentially they had missed the whole point of the Old Testament lessons.

 Ravenbrook Publishers

For a complete beginning survey of the entire Bible, see:

Mystery Revealed: A Beginner's Bible Survey

For an in-depth discussion on Creation, see:

The Bible Explains Creation

For a description of the Covenant given to Abraham, see:

Ten Keys to the Bible

For an analysis of David's kingdom and Christ's use of that plan in constructing his church, see:

The Throne of David

For putting together a hermeneutic for interpreting the Old and New Testaments, see:

A New Model for Biblical Studies

---

*These titles are available from **Ravenbrook Publishers**. You can order them and other titles on-line at **www.shenbible.org** or you can find them at your local bookstore.*

Notes

Notes

Notes

www.ingramcontent.com/pod-product-compliance
Lightning Source LLC
LaVergne TN
LVHW011355080426
835511LV00005B/295